How to Manage a Great Project

M000205283

PEARSON

At Pearson, we believe in learning – all kinds of learning for all kinds of people. Whether it's at home, in the classroom or in the workplace, learning is the key to improving our life chances.

That's why we're working with leading authors to bring you the latest thinking and best practices, so you can get better at the things that are important to you. You can learn on the page or on the move, and with content that's always crafted to help you understand quickly and apply what you've learned.

If you want to upgrade your personal skills or accelerate your career, become a more effective leader or more powerful communicator, discover new opportunities or simply find more inspiration, we can help you make progress in your work and life.

Pearson is the world's leading learning company. Our portfolio includes the Financial Times and our education business, Pearson International.

Every day our work helps learning flourish, and wherever learning flourishes, so do people.

To learn more, please visit us at **www.pearson.com/uk**

How to Manage a Great Project

On budget.
On target.
On time.

Mike Clayton

Harlow, England • London • New York • Boston • San Francisco • Toronto • Sydney • Auckland • Singapore • Hong Kong
Tokyo • Seoul • Taipei • New Delhi • Cape Town • São Paulo • Mexico City • Madrid • Amsterdam • Munich • Paris • Milan

PEARSON EDUCATION LIMITED
Edinburgh Gate
Harlow CM20 2JE
United Kingdom
Tel: +44 (0)1279 623623
Web: www.pearson.com/uk

First published 2014 (print and electronic)

© Pearson Education Limited 2014 (print and electronic)

The right of Mike Clayton to be identified as author of this work has been asserted by him in accordance with the Copyright, Designs and Patents Act 1988.

Pearson Education is not responsible for the content of third-party internet sites.

ISBN: 978-0-273-78636-8 (print)
      978-0-273-78870-6 (PDF)
      978-0-273-78869-0 (ePub)
      978-1-292-00724-3 (eText)

British Library Cataloguing-in-Publication Data
A catalogue record for the print edition is available from the British Library

Library of Congress Cataloging-in-Publication Data
Clayton, Mike.
  How to manage a great project : on budget, on target, on time / Mike Clayton.
    pages cm
  Includes bibliographical references and index.
  ISBN 978-0-273-78636-8
  1. Project management. I. Title.
  HD69.P75C522283 2014
  658.4'04--dc23
                                    2013038818

The print publication is protected by copyright. Prior to any prohibited reproduction, storage in a retrieval system, distribution or transmission in any form or by any means, electronic, mechanical, recording or otherwise, permission should be obtained from the publisher or, where applicable, a licence permitting restricted copying in the United Kingdom should be obtained from the Copyright Licensing Agency Ltd, Saffron House, 6-10 Kirby Street, London EC1N 8TS.

The ePublication is protected by copyright and must not be copied, reproduced, transferred, distributed, leased, licensed or publicly performed or used in any way except as specifically permitted in writing by the publishers, as allowed under the terms and conditions under which it was purchased, or as strictly permitted by applicable copyright law. Any unauthorised distribution or use of this text may be a direct infringement of the author's and the publishers' rights and those responsible may be liable in law accordingly.

All trademarks used herein are the property of their respective owners. The use of any trademark in this text does not vest in the author or publisher any trademark ownership rights in such trademarks, nor does the use of such trademarks imply any affiliation with or endorsement of this book by such owners.

10 9 8 7 6 5 4 3 2 1
17 16 15 14 13

Cover design by David Carroll & Co

Print edition typeset in 9/13pt Helvetica Neue LT Pro Light by 30
Printed in Great Britain by Henry Ling Ltd, at the Dorset Press, Dorchester, Dorset

NOTE THAT ANY PAGE CROSS REFERENCES REFER TO THE PRINT EDITION

To the unknown project manager
… and to all the project managers I have worked with
and trained.

May you all be favoured with the projects of your choice.
May they deliver a thousand reasons to rejoice.

(with apologies to Sheldon Harnick)

Contents

Step 7 *How is it going?*

Step 8 *How did it go?*

Learn the lingo 199

Good fortune! 205

About the author

How to Manage a Great Project is close to Mike Clayton's heart. The book has been incubating for ten years and the ideas within it go back far longer. It is a strong reflection of Mike's professional philosophy – that when you have the right process and you follow it diligently, you will put yourself in the best position to succeed. Mike has offered  this mindset to clients, colleagues and friends alike and now he finally gets the chance to offer it to you.

Mike's professional career started in consulting, after a brief spell in academic research at the University of Manchester's Physics Department. He spent much of the 1990s providing project management services to corporate and public sector clients like Railtrack, the NHS, General Motors, Vodafone, British Gas, BAA, the Ministry of Defence and Transport for London.

Since 2002, Mike has been training and coaching project managers, and delivering his powerful three-hour seminars, throughout the UK and abroad. He has also been writing books since 2008: *How to Manage a Great Project* will be his eleventh – and his third directly about project management. The other two are *Brilliant Project Leader* and *Risk Happens!*

Mike lives in Hampshire with his family.

Acknowledgements

I would like to acknowledge the fabulous learning experience I had as a project manager at Deloitte in the 1990s and, in particular, the first project management training I ever attended, which formed many of my instincts into clear ideas. I cannot recall who delivered that training, but I do recall some of the outstanding professionals I worked with at Deloitte, from whom I learned a lot. Thank you to Gilbert Toppin, Brian Green, Chris Bradley-Kidd, Keith Greig, Colin Bartle-Tubbs, Rex Mackrill, Steve Shergold and John Perry. Much of my learning was also in doing, so I would also like to acknowledge the support and encouragement I have received, particularly of clients at General Motors Germany, BAA, Vodafone and Transport for London.

Doctors are trained on a simple three-step process: see one, do one, teach one. So I would also like to acknowledge all the participants of the many thousands of hours of project management training I have delivered in the last 12 years. You are the people who gave me the opportunity to test the way I explain project management ideas and who gave me the feedback I needed to hone it. Thank you too to the clients who gave me the opportunity to train so many wonderful people. I must offer a special mention to Ron Rosenhead – a friend and mentor who gave me many of those opportunities.

Finally, thank you to my wife Felicity, who once again gave me the time to write this book and who read it cover to cover to help me find the confusing passages and silly mistakes.

How to manage a great project

Some popular project management books are witty, some are quirky. Some are filled with clever quotes and some are written for idiots.

This book is not one of them.

Instead, this book offers you certainty: certainty that, if you follow its guidance, you will feel in control of your project. It won't treat you like an idiot, but it will give you the confidence and certainty you want.

If you read and follow *How to Manage a Great Project*, it will guide you, step-by-step, through your project. It will enable you as a first-time, never-done-it-before project manager to succeed, and to deliver your project on budget, on target and on time.

And in support of that, I want to offer you a guarantee; not that you will deliver on budget, on target and on time, because there are far too many things I cannot influence that might get in the way. But what project managers crave, above all else, is control: the feeling that they know what is happening and can influence events. When you feel in control, you have a great project.

If you follow the eight simple steps in this book and, in particular, if you pay full attention to twelve essential elements, you will feel in control of your project. You will manage a great project.

That is my guarantee.

The How to Manage a Great Project Guarantee

I guarantee that when you pay full attention to these twelve things, you will feel in control of your project.

Your project goal
Your project objectives
The scope of your project
A robust case for investing
Your project plan
Your project resources
Appropriate contingency
Stakeholder communication
Prudent and active risk management
Monitoring and controlling progress
Leadership & management of your team
Control of change

This I guarantee.

Mike Clayton

How managing a great project works

Defining what we are talking about

Getting stuff done: that's what this book is about. Call it an initiative, a job, an assignment, an undertaking, an engagement, a venture or a scheme, an enterprise or a quest. Call it what you like: everybody has, at some time, to get stuff done, to make a change, to create something new.

Often, we call that a *project*.

How to recognise a project

Projects are new: they do something novel that has not been done before – or, at least, has not been done before, by you, in this place, and in this way. And they also tend to involve different steps, different materials and different people. This makes them complicated and, therefore, risky.

Lots of things need to be co-ordinated, usually to achieve a defined outcome by a specific date. Projects make change happen and produce something new and of value. To do this, there will be many tasks that need to be planned and managed and, often, there will be a limit to the amount of resources available to make all of that happen.

Whilst there are formal definitions of projects available to formal project managers (I have provided one in the chapter 'Learn the lingo'), the truth is that there are a lot of features that projects share, but many do not have all of them. Here is a checklist of those features.

Useful checklist

Is it a project or not? Ten typical features of a project

- ✔ Defined outcome, product, or thing to be produced.
- ✔ New, novel, unfamiliar or innovative – needs creative approaches.
- ✔ Clear start date.
- ✔ Clear finish date.
- ✔ Many tasks to be co-ordinated.

- ✔ Limited resources and budget.
- ✔ Different people to get involved.
- ✔ Creates change.
- ✔ Uncertainty about process or outcomes.
- ✔ Complex interdependencies among project elements or between the project and other activities.

Has what you need to do got many of these features? If it has: call it a project.

If you have a project, then *project management* is the job of making it happen.

What project management often is

Far too often, project management is a race to complete a poorly defined thing by an artificial deadline, by co-ordinating a disparate bunch of people, each of whom has their own agenda, prejudices and ideas about how to manage the chaos of a complex, novel and urgent endeavour, for which they will never be properly thanked.

Let's start again …

What project management should be

Good project management is a structured process that deals with all of the defining features of a project:

1 It defines a clear outcome.

2 It encourages creative problem-solving.

3 It manages delivery to deadlines.

4 It co-ordinates completion of tasks.

5 It makes good use of available budget and resources.

6 It engages, motivates and manages the people involved.

7 It deals with the intrinsic uncertainty and unravels the complexity.

For all of this, a project manager needs an impressive range of skills and attributes. You can develop all of these, and *How to Manage a*

Great Project will consider each of them, prioritising those that will give you the greatest sense of control over your project.

The project manager

Think of a *project manager* as a circus performer. You need to be able to keep lots of plates spinning whilst juggling many balls in the air. The plates are the streams of work that you need to keep going – the tasks. The balls are the relationships you need to constantly manage; maintaining effective communication with all the people upon whom your project depends. The tension between getting the tasks done and managing relationships will be ever-present. Perhaps your most important challenge will be to balance that tension.

THE PROJECT MANAGER

If that sounds like a job for a super man or woman, it is. There are three domains a project manager needs to pay attention to, if you are to thrive in the role and achieve the seven things that project management should do.

1 You need to be able to deploy tools and techniques that get the job done. You must be a *doer*.

2 You need to be able to impose processes and procedures that create the right amount of structure. You must be an *organiser*.

How to manage a great project

3 You need to have a helpful set of attitudes and management styles that will allow you to motivate, influence and lead your project. You must be a *succeeder*.

So let's cut out the jargon and call you what you really are: a doer, an organiser and a succeeder.

PROJECT MANAGEMENT

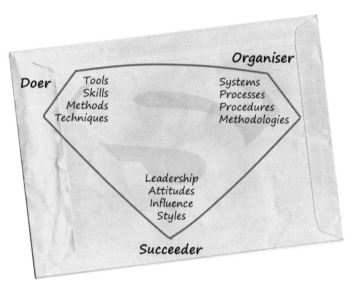

Tricks of the trade

The ideal project management temperament

How can you spot people who will thrive as project managers? There are certain personality traits that seem to favour a life working on novel and challenging projects.

1 **A balance of curiosity and caution.** Project managers need a sense of intellectual curiosity and inventiveness, but they also need to be able to maintain a level of caution and rigour, without straying towards dogma and rigidity.

2 **Efficient and organised.** Whilst a measure of easy-going never hurt anybody, too much makes for disorganised inefficiency. Projects demand a degree of discipline in bringing organisation to the complexity. ▶

3 **Outgoing and energetic.** Project management is a human endeavour and a project manager needs to be able to focus their energy on others, showing confidence, enthusiasm and resilience, and being able to assert themselves without dominating.

4 **Friendly and compassionate.** A helpful and trusting demeanour will be valuable in securing the trust and help of others. A cold, antagonistic and suspicious temperament will hardly win over sceptics and engage the support of team members.

5 **Secure and confident.** Emotional stability is vital in the roller-coaster ride that many projects can be. Project managers need to be able to remain calm and controlled in the face of adversity and deal with issues in a reasoned manner.

How projects work

From start to finish

Projects go through a number of recognisable *stages* from the first wizard-wheeze idea to the final acknowledgement that everything is done and completed. The roadmap opposite sets out the main stretches on your route. Also marked are indications of the eight steps that make up the main chapters of *How to Manage a Great Project*.

Stage 1: Define your project

The first stage is defining what your project is and what it is not. In Step 1, you will learn how to do that, because it forms the essential foundations upon which every other element of your project will be built. You will also need to establish why you are doing the project and who you are doing it for. These are Steps 2 and 3.

Stage 2: Plan your project

Once you know what your project is, the next stage is to plan it so that you know how you are going to deliver it, and also establish the critical mechanisms that you will use to stay in control in the face of adverse circumstances – as if! So Step 4 will examine how to build your plans,

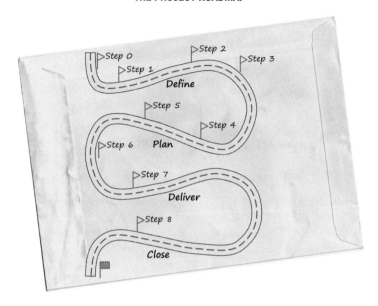

and Step 5 will look at how to involve people in delivering those plans. Step 6 is about the all-important what-ifs – what if things go wrong. So, here is where you will learn about how to spot the things that can go wrong, how to evaluate them, and what to do about them.

Stage 3: Deliver your project

Once you know what you want, why you want it and how you are going to deliver it, it is time to roll up your sleeves and make it happen. In the Delivery stage, your two principal responsibilities are to know what's going on at all times, and to act a soon as you are aware things aren't going to plan. There is plenty else to do as well, and that is all the subject of Step 7.

Stage 4: Close your project

Finally, when you have done your bit and the project has delivered the things or the changes you set out to create, your last job is to close it down in an orderly manner. This is the Closure stage, and the jobs on the last page of your to-do list are set out in Step 8.

Simple and complex projects

Project managers must, above all, be pragmatic. The projects you do will range from small to big and from simple to complex. The systems, processes and tools that project managers have developed are all enormously valuable, but not for every project. The bigger your project is, and the more complexity it has, the more of these tools you will want and the more formality you will need. Your first job is to assess how to balance the formality of more process against the flexibility of less. Then, as you proceed, keep this under review and start to identify the tools and techniques that will help you to get things done.

It is also true that bigger and more complex projects will benefit from more stages, to allow for more project-specific activities like procurement, piloting and prototyping, testing and fixing. As a project manager, you will need to assess how many and what stages will help you and your colleagues to feel in control of your project.

How to Manage a Great Project is principally written for managers of small and medium-sized projects with little or moderate complexity. My guarantee stands for bigger and more complex projects, but there are extra tools that project managers will need, to plan, monitor and control larger projects, which are outside of the scope of this book. If you are managing a small, simple project, you won't even need everything that is in this book. But I will leave you to choose which bits will work best for you.

Going from one stage to the next

Why do project managers divide their projects up into stages? The answers to this question will tell you a lot about why we use project management methods, and how they work.

Answer 1: Scheduling

Splitting a project into stages allows you to schedule each stage and get a first indication of how each part will be timed. Some project managers have a rule of thumb that the Definition and Planning stages should occupy around a half of their available time. This may seem a lot (and it won't always be right), but what they know is that plenty of time spent defining and planning your project will be repaid by knowing exactly what to do during the Delivery stage, and having far fewer unexpected glitches. Rushing through the first two stages is a rooky mistake, for which you will pay dearly later on.

Answer 2: Resourcing

Each stage is different in its nature and so will need different skills, different numbers of people, different materials and equipment and different expenditure. Dividing your project into stages allows you to start resource planning and budgeting. What we have drawn as a roadmap is often shown as a resource usage curve, where the height of the curve represents the level of resources needed at each point along the way, and the area under the curve represents the total resource needed.

PROJECT LIFECYCLE

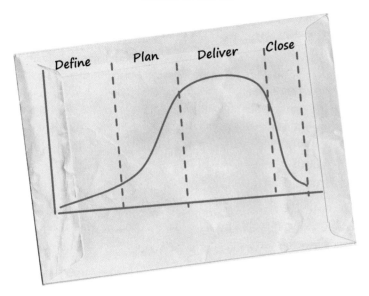

Answer 3: Momentum

Projects can be big and scary – even the smallest ones – if you are new to them. So they can be intimidating. Wouldn't it be great if you could cut them down to size? You can. By slicing them up, the first chunk can become very manageable: all that you need to do is define your project. And when you have done that, what next? Plan it.

This gives you a sense of momentum, which is one of the most powerful counters to the dread disease of procrastination. But momentum can be dangerous. You can easily find yourself caught up in the 'I've started so I'll finish' trap. But what if you start and discover problems? What if you start and, while you are working on your project, other things change, and your project is no longer the right response?

Many people reading this will have experience of projects getting started with a lot of fanfare and then, months later, people are wondering why. Things have changed and now people are asking: 'What are we wasting our money, our time, our commitment on this for? It's a waste.' Yet the project continues and then, when it delivers its goods, nobody knows what they are for. They are no longer needed or wanted. They are ignored: reports shelved, assets stored, procedures abandoned before they are ever used.

Answer 4: Control

You need to stop that happening. The fourth answer to the question: 'Why do we have stages?' is not about the stages at all: it is about the *boundaries* between them. At each boundary, we can exert control. We change the presumption from continuing to stopping. Before we continue, we need to be satisfied that it is still the right thing to do. So we ask two questions:

1 **Look backwards:** 'Have we completed everything we need to have in place to consider this stage done?' If we have, we ask …

2 **Look forwards:** 'Having learned what we have learned and, considering anything that has changed since our last review, is it still the right thing to do to continue?'

> **Mike's rules**
>
> The one thing a project manager craves, above all else, is control.

This go/no-go decision creates crucial accountability and control. In particular, we ask specific questions at the end of each stage:

How to manage a great project

STAGE BOUNDARIES

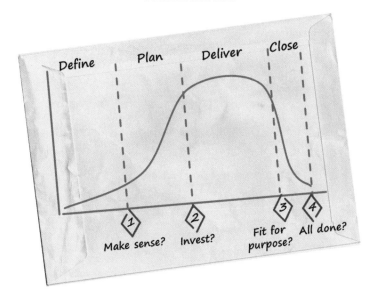

→ **Boundary 1: Does this project make sense?** Is it consistent with everything else you want to do, is it ethical and lawful, is it likely to succeed, and does it look like good value for money?

→ **Boundary 2: Should we invest?** Now you have a plan, detailed specifications and, as a result, a final budget. Do you believe you can deliver the project and, if you do, will you get a good return on your investment of time, commitment and money?

→ **Boundary 3: Is what we have produced fit for purpose?** Once you have delivered the things, processes, ideas or whatever else you set up the project for, do they meet the needs of the people who commissioned them? If they do, they will accept them from you, the project manager, and be prepared to pay for them. If they don't, they won't and you will have to fix them.

→ **Boundary 4: Are we all done?** Have you finished the project, handed it over and closed it down in an orderly fashion? If you have, that's it; you're done. It is time to go home and relax. You have done well, so there will inevitably be another project coming soon.

More stages and stage boundaries

Where your project is more complex, you may want more control points. This is easily achieved by adding additional stages and stage boundaries. Common examples are:

→ Creating a pilot phase between planning and delivery to build and evaluate a prototype solution and refine designs and plans accordingly.

→ Creating test and remediation stages after delivery and before handover. Technology projects often have several stages of testing and remediation; testing individual components first (component testing), then testing them all together (integration testing), and then letting users test them in realistic scenarios (user testing).

→ Planning a complex project may involve several stages, moving from initial outline plans to final detailed plans.

→ You may need to procure services, materials or assets and might therefore want a separate stage for procurement – or even several stages for defining the brief, tendering and contract negotiation.

→ Including a post-implementation review stage, after formal closure of your project, to assess how well it has bedded into your organisation's processes and culture.

Tricks of the trade

S curves

Project managers like diagrams, and one of the most telling of all is the resource depletion curve. In the top figure opposite, the solid curve represents the total resources used – whether it is team members' time, materials or budget. The dashed curve therefore represents the resources that remain. It is sometimes called a resource depletion curve.

At the start of the project you have plenty of resources and you are not using them up too quickly. You have time to plan – just as a skier at the top of a mountain has plenty of time to select their best route to the bottom.

But once the skier starts down the slope, they move quickly, with little time to plan and prepare. They must react quickly and every choice they make has profound consequences. They rapidly use up their options.

RESOURCE UTILISATION

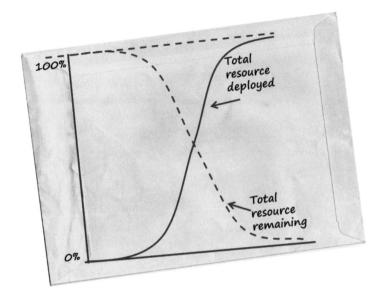

RESOURCE DEPLETION

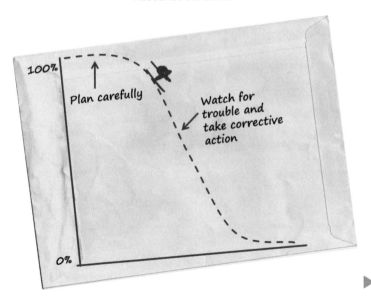

You too will start to use up your resources faster and faster. During the Delivery stage, resources will rapidly deplete. Changes will be harder and more costly to make, and will create greater risk to your eventual success. Most of your time will be spent looking out for trouble and trying to put it right. If you want to feel in control during the rapid descent of the Delivery stage, you must plan carefully, while you have the chance. The foundations of your project's success (or not) are in Steps 1 to 6.

A guide to How to Manage a Great Project

So, now you understand the stages and steps in a project, let's review the eight steps that make up the main chapters of this book, and the two chapters that will end it.

How to Manage a Great Project works on a very simple basis:

> ### Mike's rules
>
> When you have a sound process, trust it. Follow it, do it well, stick with it.

Step 1: What do you want?

One of the main reasons we fail to achieve what we set out to do is not being clear enough what success looks like. So Step 1 is to define your initiative or project with clarity and precision, defining success and being clear what it is for.

Step 2: Does it stack up?

Does your project make sense? Success can only come if what you are trying to do is worthwhile, so Step 2 requires you to assess the pros and cons of your initiative and be able to convince yourself and others that it is truly worthwhile.

Step 3: Who cares?

Who gets to determine whether you have been successful or not? There will be a whole range of people, and maybe groups and institutions, who have an interest in what you are doing. How will you win their support and commitment, and counter any resistance or opposition you meet?

Step 4: How will you get what you want?

Planning and preparation are everything. There is a whole host of tools available to you that are neither difficult to use nor require special equipment or software. In Step 4, we'll look at how you can give yourself and others the confidence that you know what you are doing and you have the resources you need.

Step 5: Who will help?

Aside from you, who else needs to be involved in your project? How will you allocate work, secure guidance and support, and ensure people collaborate well and take responsibility for their portion of work? Step 5 will also show you how to secure co-operation and ensure that people meet their commitments to you.

Step 6: What if it goes wrong?

You can be certain that things will go wrong … but what things? It's time to foresee trouble, assess the risks and figure out how to deal with them in a pragmatic and efficient manner. This is the discipline of risk management, and it is central to managing a great project.

Step 7: How is it going?

You need to understand how to stay in control of what you are doing during the times when things are changing at their fastest. You know that shift happens and things go wrong, so how can you deal with it effectively and respond to a range of typical problems?

Step 8: How did it go?

Your project went well – you delivered the goods: congratulations! Now wrap it up in an orderly manner.

Learn the lingo

What you have learned in this book is all of the fundamentals of project management. Now let's put the language, jargon and formality to it, so that you can start to call yourself a project manager. Alternatively, if you are happy calling yourself a doer, an organiser and a succeeder, then just skip this chapter!

Good fortune!

A brief closing section, to wish you well.

A word about the sample templates in the 'Organising yourself' sections

How to Manage a Great Project contains practical templates that you can use quickly and easily to capture project information and to help you with controlling your project. To fit them more easily on to the page, standard project information, which would appear on all templates, has been omitted. This includes the names of the project, the project manager and sponsor, and space for authorisation and status details.

Each of these templates is also available for you to download and adapt to your own needs, from **www.manageagreatproject.co.uk**. These versions contain space for all of that information and are laid out with more room for you to enter information. There are also further templates to download, also free.

Lessons from the real world

1 Project managers with greater flexibility tend to have an easier time getting things done and tend to get better results.

2 Make sure that you believe the project has a realistic chance of success before you say 'yes' to managing it. Project managers need to be able to say 'no' – and it starts before Step 1.

What do you want?

Step 1

Essential practices of Step 1

1 Research and analyse the opportunity or need.

2 Evaluate prior lessons learned.

3 Define your goal and objectives.

4 Define your scope of work, list of deliverables and specifications.

5 Establish the project stages and gateway procedures.

Before you start: Step Zero

Something needs to get done. Things are not as they should be, or someone has spotted a chance to improve things. And you have been identified as the person to make it all happen. The first step in our project management process is to decide what, precisely, needs to be done, but to prepare for that, there are some things to do before you start: Step Zero.

Step Zero is about taking an inventory of where you are before you start, and what you know.

Where are you now?

Make sure you have as much understanding as possible of the context within which your project will sit. What is the challenge that needs to be addressed and why? What is to be gained by making the improvements and what is in place already? This will all lead you towards an understanding of the nature of the opportunity or of the need.

If you think about this in terms of building and construction, this is like conducting a survey of the ground or the existing building. Include in your survey elements of history and what people have learned from previous experiences, personalities and relationships, assets and problems. What you need to know and what you can find out will depend entirely on your context: at the simplest, this is about asking questions.

What do you know?

Keep asking questions to find what assumptions people are making – especially those that are made without people realising that they are nothing but assumptions. These unacknowledged assumptions can pose a big risk to your project. Find out what has already been tried or done, how it worked out and what was learned from those experiences. And start to gauge the social and political environment.

What goes wrong?

A common source of project failure is either when goals and objectives are unclear, or when they are disconnected from the organisation's other priorities. In the first case, you risk confusion during design, planning and delivery, and the possibility of producing something of little value. In the second case, the deliverables will not serve the organisation well and may result in undesirable unintended consequences.

What do you want?

The starting place for defining your project is the question:

What do you want?

The answer to this question is your *goal*: the aim of your project. If you are doing something for yourself, take time to think this through carefully and to discuss it with other people whose opinions you value.

More likely, you are doing the project for someone else, or for an organisation. So you may need to ask the question of a number of people, starting with the person who is commissioning the project. What is important here is to understand the range of views that you will hear and to work with those people to generate a single statement that everyone can agree to. This can take a while, but do not shy away from exposing disagreements, or take the easy route of settling for an imprecise answer that is easy to agree on.

One way to establish whether you do have a good statement of the goal is to ask:

What is the purpose of doing this?

If everyone agrees that the purpose is worthwhile and also that the goal you have articulated is the best way of achieving that purpose, then you have a good goal.

How to word your goal

The goal is the overarching definition of what your project is about, so it is a good idea to spend some time refining the wording. Firstly, it needs to be crystal clear and unambiguous, so that nobody will easily misunderstand it. But it also needs to be motivating. When you are encouraging other people to support you, or even to help out, the goal will be the answer to their question 'What are you doing?'

So, for example, your goal could be 'To build a greenhouse', or it could equally be 'To build a greenhouse that will create an environment to grow healthy, sustainable food for my family'. Both may be accurate but the second version also contains a purpose, which is better for two reasons:

1 It will help guide you in making decisions, such as: how big, what layout, what specifications?

2 It will help to motivate people to help you, because they will understand why you are doing it and, if the reason appeals to them, they will want to help.

The greenhouse project

Goal: To build a greenhouse that will create an environment to grow healthy, sustainable food for my family.

How do you want it?

You are going to do your project so you can achieve your goal. But there are going to be more criteria that you or others will use to judge whether you are successful or not. These may be about whether you have built your greenhouse in time for planting your vegetables, whether you have built it properly, whether it provides the right environment for the vegetables you intend to grow, or whether you have spent more or less money than you intended to. When you know *what* you want to achieve, the next question to ask is:

How do you want it?

The answer to this establishes some important constraints on your project and what you consider success to look like. These fall into three categories: *time*, *cost* and *quality*. They are usually shown as three corners of the *time–cost–quality (TCQ) triangle*.

THE TIME–COST–QUALITY TRIANGLE

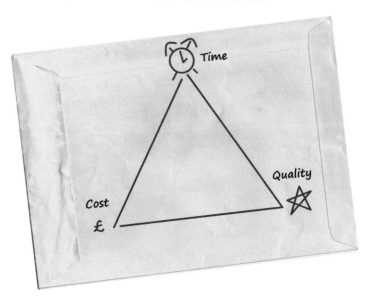

Typically, one of these three dimensions will be more important than the others for your project. Your requirements for time (schedule), cost (budget) and quality (specification) will be your *objectives*.

Some projects are time-driven, with a clear deadline for completion which results from externally generated constraints. Examples of these constraints could include legislative or regulatory deadlines, anniversaries or an announcement by someone prominent.

Some projects are quality-driven. It is critical to the promoters that certain quality standards are met. The three commonest reasons for this are: to provide assurance of required functionality, to comply with health and safety requirements, or to protect a reputation.

Projects can also be cost-driven, which is the case where you are given a fixed budget with no likelihood of any further funds. So you must bring it in on budget come what may – even if that means a delay or compromising quality. Many people instantly assume that their project is cost-driven when, in fact, they are making a lazy assumption about their organisation. Most organisations require projects to conform to specific quality or schedule constraints and then require the project manager to 'optimise for cost' – to keep costs as low as you can, given the other constraints.

A good way to facilitate a consistent answer to the question 'How do you want it?' is to draw a TCQ triangle and get the people who matter to indicate, with a cross, where they see the project's priorities. For example, our greenhouse project may merit a cross near to the quality corner.

THE TIME–COST–QUALITY TRIANGLE: PRIORITY

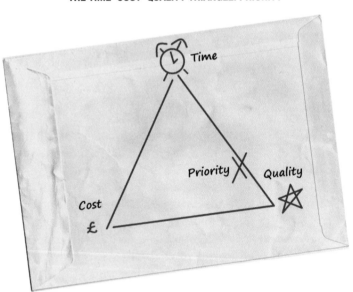

The greenhouse project

Objectives:

1 To build a greenhouse that has toughened glass, a minimum area of 11 m^2, and with fully galvanised supports to ensure long life.

2 To complete all work, ready for use by 28 February.

How to manage a great project

This recognises that getting it right is most important, but secondary is the desire to get it ready in time for planting in early March. Note that cost is the least important objective in this example. If you were to cost out the materials and labour, and schedule the work, you would develop a budget, which would fix the cost. Now the three corners of your triangle are set.

If you wanted to bring work forward, to be ready mid-February, you can, but you will either have to spend a little extra on labour or cut corners. Once the TCQ triangle is fixed, the three corners constrain one another. It is often also called the *triple constraint* or the *triangle of balance* for this reason. If you want to save money, you can, if you go for lower quality materials or poorer workmanship and, if you want a better greenhouse, you will need to pay more and maybe also take longer building it.

You can trade the three constraints off against one another, but you can never get something for nothing. Knowing where the cross is, and hence what your priorities are, will help you make decisions when shift happens and something goes wrong.

Precision objectives

Your TCQ objectives define success for your project. Achieving them all is complete success: missing one or more is not – even when you do achieve your goal. Therefore, you need to state your requirements for time (schedule), cost (budget) and quality (specification) as precisely as you can. Here is a checklist to help you.

Useful checklist
The triple SR

Make sure that your objectives are *triple SR*:

- ✔ **Strategic.** Are they strategically relevant and aligned to your own or your organisation's wider goals and objectives?
- ✔ **Recorded.** Have you recorded your objectives so that they are widely known and transparent to all stakeholders?
- ✔ **Specific.** Are the objectives objectively measurable and can progress against them be readily tracked?

▶

- ✔ **Realistic.** Can they be realistically achieved and the goal be delivered to the budget, schedule and specification set?
- ✔ **Stretching.** Have you set ambitious and challenging objectives that will deliver real value or have you just made life easy for yourself?
- ✔ **Responsible.** Are the objectives and goal compliant; environmentally, ethically and legally?

Keep something up your sleeve

If your TCQ objectives tell you what is least important then, when something goes wrong, you will know what to compromise on – in our example, budget. The only problem with this is that sometimes, despite having clear priorities, when you go to the person who has commissioned you to do the project – your boss, your client, your partner, maybe – their answer is 'no'. You cannot have extra money; nor can you have more time, nor can you cut corners.

Prudent project managers will have something to spare in their back pocket. They will have sought a little more budget than they thought

THE TIME–COST–QUALITY TRIANGLE: SCOPE

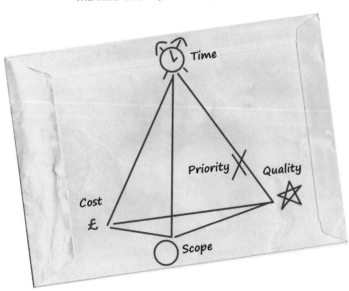

How to manage a great project

they would need, just in case. They would have scheduled just a little more time than their plan said they would need, just in case. And they would have set out quality standards that were a bit higher than strictly necessary, just in case. This is *contingency*.

But what happens when you have run out of contingency? You have no more time, budget or corners to cut? That is when, like a great performer, you need something up your sleeve, as well.

It's like the TCQ triangle has a fourth corner, and that corner is *scope*.

How much of it do you want?

Scope answers another question:

How much of it do you want?

Scope is a statement of the breadth and depth of your ambition for the project. It is a description of everything that the project needs to do. It is easy to represent scope as a diagram.

SCOPE

In the diagram, everything inside the circle is 'in scope'. It is the work of the project to produce it: it is your job. Everything outside the project is 'out of scope': it is not your concern. It may be important, but somebody else or some other project will take care of it, or it may not be important enough, and it is not needed. Defining the scope of your project is, perhaps, the hardest single part of project management. We will return to how to do it in the section 'Putting it all together', later in this chapter, and how to articulate it formally in the chapter 'Step 4: How will you get what you want?' For now, let's concentrate on understanding more about what scope is.

There are two ways that you can think about scope. Each is equally useful, but it is best to choose one and stick to it for your project. In the UK, scope is most often thought of as the work that needs to get done; the tasks that the project must undertake. We talk about 'the scope of work'. In the USA, project managers are more likely to speak of scope as referring to the things the project produces; the products of the work you do. The two formulations will produce the same result in the end, as long as you either do all of the work, or produce all of the things. But it is best not to mix the two up, because doing one piece of work may produce one physical product – or none – or two. You may need to do two or three or more pieces of work to produce a physical thing. This lack of one-to-one relationship means that mixing the two can get you into an awful mess. Stick to one. In this book, we will choose to think of scope as the work to be done.

The greenhouse project

Scope:
→ Preparing the ground to accommodate a greenhouse.
→ Preparing a path to the greenhouse site.
→ Research, purchase and assembly of one greenhouse.
→ Putting in all the glass.
→ Fitting out the greenhouse with working surfaces and ventilation.

There always elements of choice in deciding scope, which is what makes it so difficult.

Scope creep

There are three words that project managers have come to fear above all others. Once you have a project, you have materials, equipment, people and a budget. People can smell those, and they smell good. You will also be creating something new, and maybe innovating too. That attracts people. So they will sniff out your project, they will see within it an opportunity, and they will approach you, the project manager, and flatter you. And then, they will speak those three words. They will say 'While you are doing this project …' here they come:

Could you just …

'Could you just' is their attempt to get their agenda included in your project. Which, from their point of view, is perfectly reasonable. But from your point of view, they are asking you to commit your people, your resources, your time and energy to delivering what they want – as well as what you are supposed to be doing. They are trying to expand the boundaries of your project; a process known as *scope creep*.

SCOPE CREEP

What goes wrong?

The danger with scope creep, if you allow it, is that you will divert your resources to doing what they want and compromise your ability to deliver your project at the same time. You must stop scope creep. It is insidious and one of the principal threats to a project.

To stop it, you must first understand why it happens. There are a number of reason; not least, opportunism; maybe also meanness, or possibly foolishness. But the commonest reason is simple misunderstanding. People's interpretation of the boundary of your scope is different to yours; what you think of as out of scope will, to them, seem like it is clearly in scope. This happens because the boundary is fuzzy and too poorly defined.

In our example, you are part way through building the greenhouse when you get the question: 'What sort of heater are you putting in it?' Heater? You aren't going to put in a heater. That is not part of your scope. Yet to some people, 'fitting it out' means putting in a heater. To you, it just means shelves and racks. You each have a different understanding of the scope.

So, to manage scope creep, there are two things you must do.

Define your scope with precision

You must be as clear and precise as you can about what is in scope, and also what is out of scope. Use your judgement and experience – and the judgement and experience of those around you – to identify those things which others may assume are in scope, but which are not. Document these exclusions explicitly as out of scope, alongside your documentation of what is in scope.

The greenhouse project

Out of scope:

→ Providing heating for the greenhouse.

→ Providing consumable materials, like planters, pots, soil and sand.

→ Planting or any other horticultural activities.

Get your definition of scope signed off

When you have fully documented your scope, take that document to the person or people for whom you are doing the project. Ask them to review your scope statements carefully. If they will be satisfied when you do everything you have documented as in scope and nothing that you have documented as out of scope, then ask them to sign your scope statement to authorise it.

DEALING WITH SCOPE CREEP

Your authorised statement of scope is ammunition you need to reject attempts for scope creep. 'Sorry,' you can say, 'but I can't do that. My boss or client has signed this to say that I must not.' And even if they play that game called 'autograph top-trumps' and say 'Ah, but my boss's signature trumps yours', you are still in a strong position. With a clearly defined scope, you have a firm base for negotiating the impact of additional scope on your resources and timescales.

Tricks of the trade
Outputs or outcomes?

The things that the project produces, like physical things, new processes or events, are known as *products* or *deliverables* (things the project delivers). They are also sometimes called *outputs*, although this term derives less from project management than from the way organisations describe processes in general.

These are different, however, to *outcomes*, which are the changes that happen as a result of the project. In our example, a greenhouse is the deliverable, product or output from our project. The outcomes are supplies of fresh produce, a healthier diet, perhaps, or reduced shopping bills. Whilst the output is what the project manager is focused on achieving, the outcomes are the real reason for doing the project.

When you are deciding your goal, objectives and scope, consider both outputs and outcomes. You will need to describe the outputs clearly – that is the job of the project. You may also want to set out the outcomes, to make sure the outputs are well-chosen and designed to generate the desired outcomes.

What does it need to look like?

Once you have the scope settled, the next question to resolve, for each thing you need to produce, is:

What does it need to look like?

The answer to this question is the *specification* for each deliverable: the size of your greenhouse, its layout, the type of glass, the material that the frame will be made out of, how many vents it will have, what sort of base it will sit on …

The greenhouse project

Specification:

→ Size: 4.5 m x 2.8 m

→ Frame material: aluminium

> ➔ Plinth: galvanised steel, 12 cm high
>
> ➔ Base: concrete slab 5.5 m x 3.4 m
>
> ➔ Glass: toughened safety glass

The specification will define the tiniest details of your project. As we have moved from aim to objectives to scope to specification, it has been as if we have been peeling the layers of an onion, examining ever-finer details.

LAYERS OF DETAIL

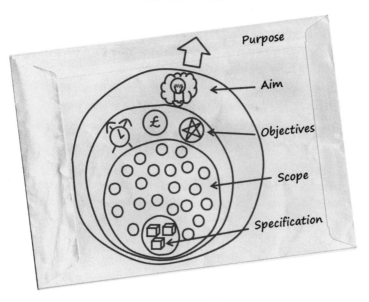

Detailing the requirements

To develop your specification, you need to start by documenting the *requirements* that different people will have for your products. Remember that each requirement you add will need to be traded off against additional cost and time. Some requirements are scope-related (typically, functionality and often security and compliance), whilst the others (sometimes called non-functional requirements) are more about quality.

Useful checklist
Ten types of requirement

✔ **Functionality.** What does it need to be able to do, and how must it do it?

✔ **Usability.** How easy does it need to be to use?

✔ **Performance standards.** How well does it need to be able to do what it does? This could be about speed, error rates or, in the example of our greenhouse, thermal gain – how much warmer will it be inside compared to outside?

✔ **Reliability.** Everything degrades, so how much time between failures or planned maintenance do you need to design in? Reliability is often described in terms either of *mean time to failure* or *percentage availability*.

✔ **Maintenance.** How easy or difficult, expensive or cheap is it to maintain, and how often will it need scheduled maintenance?

✔ **Documentation.** What documentation will you need to provide for the owner and user, to support them once you have handed over your project?

✔ **Compliance.** What legal, regulatory or quality standards must it comply with?

✔ **Safety.** A particular example of compliance requirements that you will often need to consider.

✔ **Security.** Whether it is physical security (a lock on your greenhouse) or something more abstract like keeping data confidential, security is often a compliance requirement, but often sits outside of regulatory frameworks and so is a preference.

✔ **Environmental.** Another example of a requirement that is now often regulated and thus a part of compliance. You may choose to set a zero carbon requirement on heating your greenhouse, so avoid kerosene: wind, photo-voltaic or ground source heat may be your solution.

Finding all these requirements and then turning them into a specification is an essential component of designing your project. You will need to consult with a variety of people and may find that some of their perspectives conflict with one another.

With the most important people, you will want to sit down and discuss their requirements with them. For others, you may want to speak to them in small groups or maybe issue questionnaires in one form or another. Paper questionnaires are simple, but for very big groups consider online questionnaire tools, which save you the job of entering the answers on to a database to help analyse them. You may also want to observe users using any predecessor assets, visit sites with successful installations and conduct desk research.

The end product of requirements gathering will be a statement of everything you have learned in *MoSCoW* format:

Musts: Essential items: the project will fail without them. These are sometimes referred to as the MUST: Minimum Usable SubseT.

Shoulds: High priority items that supplement the Musts. These can be dropped if either: they are not truly essential, they can be delayed, or an alternative means of satisfying the requirement is available.

Coulds: Low priority items that are 'nice to have'. These will often be developed if the cost is marginal and an important person pushes for them. They are the easiest part of scope to drop, if shift happens and there is a problem, with no additional time or budget to spare.

Won'ts: The lowest priority items, which we'd like to do but cannot justify the expense, risk or delay. We would if we could: but we won't.

Your decisions about what goes into which category will often be political ones, deciding on which people to please and which to disappoint. This is one of the reasons that scoping is so difficult!

Mike's rules

You can please all of your stakeholders, some of the time ... and you can please some of your stakeholders all of the time ... but you will not be able to please all of your stakeholders all of the time.

Tricks of the trade
Agreeing your MoSCoW list

One way to ease the development of a final list is to gather people together in a room. Put four posters up, marked Musts, Shoulds, Coulds and Won'ts. Write each requirement on a sticky note and work with the group to agree what goes where. Start with the Musts.

When you are close to agreement, impose a one-in/one-out policy on the Shoulds, only accepting one transfer from Coulds to Shoulds when it is balanced by another move from Shoulds down to Coulds. This will reduce the scale of scope inflation.

Thinking about quality

There are three stages to getting quality right on a project, which occur at three of our steps.

Quality design

Occurs at Step 1, discussed here …

Quality design is about creating specifications and a design that match the quality requirements. They meet any externally set quality standards and compliance requirements, and also balance people's ideals with a realistic view of the budget and the marginal cost of additional quality.

Quality assurance

Planned at Step 4 and implemented at Step 7, discussed at Step 4.

Quality assurance is a process you establish to ensure that everything you produce meets its quality design specification. This is about how you do things day-to-day and how you check your work as you go along.

Quality control

Implemented throughout Step 7.

When something is finished, *quality control* is the process of checking that it matches its specification, and the resultant remedial actions if it does not. This is your last chance to protect your reputation.

Putting it all together

Putting together your goal, objective, scope and specification creates a full project definition. We usually document this in what is sometimes called a *project definition document*. It can also be known as a *project charter*, a *project brief*, *project terms of reference* or an *outline project initiation document* (PID). This document allows you to test your understanding of what you have been told, to present it to others for their confirmation and, once confirmed, it becomes the foundational document of your project.

What else goes into a project definition document?

By the end of your project Definition stage, your definition document will need to contain statements of your goal, objectives and scope. As you move through the Planning stage, your scope statement will be more robust. We will see (in Step 4) how a powerful tool called a *work breakdown* will allow you to articulate your scope completely, item by item.

Your definition also needs to contain a list of deliverables from your project. These too will be refined at the Planning stage, where you will also add detailed specifications and standards for each one.

The purpose of your project definition is to help you and your decision makers to evaluate your project and determine whether it merits the additional investment of time, effort and resources to specify, plan and justify it fully at the Planning stage. This will be the first go/no-go decision. More information will help with that purpose, so we normally include the following in our project definition document:

Dependencies and constraints

What other activities or initiatives will your project connect to, creating a dependency – in terms of matters like scheduling, shared resources, decision making or the provision of deliverables from one project to the other? And what constraints limit your choices on the project? In our greenhouse example, building a new garage at around the same time may offer the chance to share equipment and supplies, if you plan the timing appropriately: this is a dependency. There may only be one site in the garden where you can put your greenhouse: this is a constraint.

Assumptions, risks and uncertainties

Early on in defining your project there will be much that you do not know. To make progress, you must therefore make *assumptions*. The danger with assumptions is not when we make them, but when we forget that they are only assumptions, rather than something we know. Each assumption therefore carries with it the risk that it is flawed. Assumptions, risks and uncertainties are three aspects of the same thing. For example, you might assume that the weather in late February will be suitable for laying a concrete slab on which to site your greenhouse; in fact, weather will always be an *uncertainty* and there is a consequent *risk* that it will be too cold for the concrete to set properly.

At the Definition stage of your project, you need to identify the big assumptions, risks and uncertainties that could cause your project to fail. Any that remain as you enter the Planning stage will become your priority to resolve by testing the assumption, planning the risk out of your project or resolving the uncertainty. We shall return to this at Step 6.

Issues

An *issue* is a known problem that needs to be resolved. Approval to proceed at a stage boundary will be subject to resolution of any known issues, so it is important to be open about what you are aware of. If you are not, and it later emerges that you were aware of the issues, you could reasonably be held accountable for any impact that the issue has: potentially the failure of the project.

A fundamental principle of good project management is openness and honesty about problems. Your job as a project manager is to expose problems, understand them and find solutions. Your decision makers need to understand those problems, not just so that they can make better-informed decisions, but so that they can support you with guidance and advice, and also with decisions that will enable you to act. We will consider this in more detail in 'Step 7: How is it going?' – where we examine the delivery phase and how to handle the problems that arise when things do not go according to plan.

Approach

Your project definition document needs to indicate the broad *approach* you will take to delivering your project. This is far from being a plan (which we shall cover in 'Step 4: How will you get what you want?') but does give decision makers an indication of your overall strategy, answering questions like:

→ Will you do the work yourself or contract it out?

→ Will it be phased or done in one go?

→ Will you use experimental ideas or stick with highly trusted methods?

→ Will you use a standard 'off-the-shelf' solution or create a customised one?

The other vital aspect of approach to consider is the broad structure of your project. What are the stages you will need? Simple projects may have just the four we are using, but you may need more. You will also need to define the tests to be set at stage boundaries and who will make the go/no-go decisions.

Benefits and budget estimate

The go/no-go decision must be informed by an assessment of what the project will cost and what the customer, client or owner will get in return for their investment. Remember from the last chapter that the question that must be answered at the first stage boundary is 'Does this project make sense?' To answer this, we will need to know not just what the project is and is not (its definition), but also whether it is aligned with other things you or your organisation plan to do and whether, in doing it, it will represent good value for money.

At the Definition stage, you will not have the detail needed to spell out all the benefits or to calculate a detailed budget. Here, you will be looking for the main reasons for doing the project and the broad costs of the major items, with a chunk of extra money to cover smaller, unidentified, costs and contingencies.

This will start to answer the question of whether your project stacks up as a project. It is such an important question that the whole of the next step, 'Step 2: Does it stack up?' is devoted to it.

Tricks of the trade

A name for your project

Giving your project a name makes it easier for people to talk about it. Your choice of name can make it easy for people to quickly understand what it is about or give it an air of mystery. The name can be playful or serious, emotive or abstract. Whatever you choose, make sure it is easy to pronounce – which is a particular challenge for large projects that involve people with different first languages – and does not offer unintended and unwelcome interpretations.

Here are seven ideas:

1 Random, unexpected and ambiguous project names create a sense of intrigue that gets people interested in trying to figure out why you chose the name. It is also a good approach for secret projects. If the name is genuinely random, it will not help people to guess what is going on. This is how the UK police name their operations: the names are picked randomly from a list, so that they have no connection with the case. Examples include Bumblebee, Ore, Arundel, and Julie.

2 Metaphors and analogies are good ways to remind people of something important about your project. Project Trident may have three key features. Project Unity may be designed to bring two teams together into one new one.

3 Mythology and literature provide a near infinite array of well-known characters and events to name your project after. Project Theseus might be about overcoming a powerful competitor, for example. Examples of hard-to-pronounce names abound here, however. Adopting the name Project Quetzalcoatl to indicate fertility may make good sense as a metaphor, but some people will find the name hard to say and remember.

4 Acronyms can be playful or clever (NASA is fond of them – from Arctic Composition Explorer – ACE, to the Wide-field Infra-red Survey Explorer – WISE). They can also be confusing and obscure the project.

5 Name your project after something that has the properties that you want people to attach to your project: Project Rolls Royce if you want people to associate luxury and elegance with your project, or Project Lightning if speed is the association you want.

6 Conjure up emotions with a name like Project Discovery, Project Happiness or Project Service.

7 Choose a name that says what your project does, like Project Greenhouse.

Organising yourself

On the page overleaf is a sample template for your project definition document. You can download a copy, which you can adapt to your own needs, from **www.manageagreatproject.co.uk**

Negotiating your project definition document

Preparing a project definition document is rarely a simple desk exercise. You will have a lot of people who will have an interest in the decisions you make about what precisely you set as your goal, what objectives you set and what you conclude will be in and out of scope. This means you will need to enter into a series of discussions and negotiations that may need several rounds of refinement.

There will rarely be right or wrong answers – just the ones that best fit the situation and, in a given situation, different project managers may make different choices. This is especially so with what to put into and out of scope, when choosing from the 'shoulds' and 'coulds'. Which people to please and which to disappoint may be challenging both intellectually and emotionally.

Mike's rules

Scoping is the most difficult part of project management.

Your negotiation and conflict management skills will come to the fore here, so we will highlight these in 'Step 3: Who cares?' when we discuss stakeholder communication skills.

Project definition template

Project goal	*What do you want? What is the project about, what is its purpose, what benefits will it produce?*
Project objectives	*What are the criteria against which project success will be measured? Include any time, cost or quality targets. Think about the triple SR framework for effective objectives.*
Project scope	*What will be the overall 'size' of the proposed project, and what areas/work will it include?*
Exclusions	*What tasks, activities and related outcomes are out of scope?*
Requirements	*The essential requirements that the project must meet for the customer to accept it. At this stage, criteria may not be fully known or quantifiable, so indicate the basis for acceptance.*
Project deliverables	*Key products, or end results, which the project will deliver (e.g. new computer system, trained staff, policy guidance).*
Dependencies and constraints	*What external considerations might impact on the project? What other activities will this project be dependent upon? What relationships are there with other projects, programmes and procedures?*
Assumptions, risks and uncertainties	*What assumptions have you made in preparing this project definition? What are the risks to the project? What do you not yet know?*
Approach	*What approach will you take to delivering your project? (For example, procurement, quality and regulated matters.)*
Quality	*How will you make sure that you get quality right?*
Equality and diversity	*How will the project maximise the benefits to all potential users? What legislative/regulatory requirements should be considered?*
Health and safety	*What health and safety issues are likely to arise and how will they be managed?*
Costs	*What are the broad areas of the project budget? What is your current best estimate of cost, and your level of confidence? How much contingency do you need?*
Benefits	*What benefits will the project bring? Include quantifiable financial benefits and non-financial benefits.*

Lessons from the real world

1 Never ever start a project unless you know what you are trying to achieve and therefore what success will look like.

2 Get all of your assumptions out in the open, so that you and your team can examine and test each one. Where you cannot resolve an assumption, consider the alternative scenario: that the opposite assumption may be true. What would that do to your project?

3 Don't be impatient to move past defining your project. This step is so important; without it, your project has no compass bearing to follow and you'll end up wandering around randomly.

4 When your boss (or your client) agrees your project definition, get a signature. Make them physically confirm that this is what they want.

5 If you don't know what 'done' looks like when you start delivering your project, you may find you never stop.

6 If you have too many goals, that may be a sign that you really have two or more projects scrambled up together. Separating them out will make it easier and less risky.

Does it stack up?

Step 2

Essential practices of Step 2

1 Evaluate your investment in the project: should you invest?

Balancing pros and cons

At the boundaries between each stage of your project, you need to secure a go/no-go decision. Between the first stage, Defining your project, and the second stage, Planing your project, that decision is based on the question:

Does this project make sense?

You need to evaluate what the project is and is not (its definition) and consider the extent to which it is consistent with what your organisation wants to achieve: its strategic objectives and its current priorities. If your project is consistent, then you must also consider the extent to which it appears to offer good value for money.

At the Definition stage, this is tricky. You don't have enough information to fully assess its costs and benefits: much detail is still missing. You need to answer the question 'Does it stack up?' in broad terms, preparing what is called an *outline investment appraisal*.

Once you enter the Planning stage, you can start work on improving the precision and detail of your specification, on building plans for implementation of your project and putting detailed costs to that plan. What will emerge will be a fully costed plan that becomes your project budget. When you set that against a careful evaluation of the project's benefits, you can build a *full investment appraisal* to answer the question posed at the boundary at the end of the Planning stage:

Should we invest?

As with defining your project (in Step 1) and much else that follows, you will be starting work on showing whether your project stacks up at the earliest stages of your project, refining your assessment all the way up to the end of the Planning stage, and then keeping it under review through your Delivery stage.

What is an investment appraisal?

Think of an *investment appraisal* as the scales of justice, balancing all the reasons to do your project – the benefits and advantages – against all the reasons not to do it – the costs and risks.

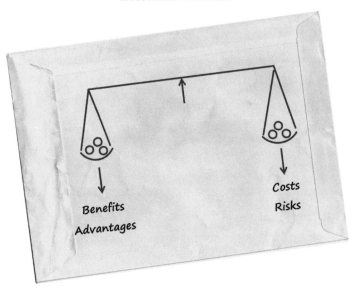

A full investment appraisal will provide this comparison for your project, as proposed, and also for a range of variants on your project, offering alternative solutions. This will allow your decision makers to select the one that is best for the organisation, balancing not only cost and benefit, but also resource availability.

An investment appraisal makes use of a variety of tools from the simple *force-field analysis* of comparing pros and cons, to sophisticated financial modelling called *discounted cash flow analysis.*

What is a business case?

A *business case* is what most organisations use to justify – or make the case for – a project. Whilst an investment appraisal sets out a fair assessment of the evidence, a business case is a piece of advocacy. It develops the case to demonstrate why you should undertake a project. The investment appraisal then becomes a part of your business case, which sets out the comparison of pros and cons to make the case.

You are far more likely to be asked to prepare a business case, to justify your project, than to be asked for a more neutral investment appraisal. The checklist below sets out the principal components of a business case.

Useful checklist

Sample structure for a full business case

Make the level of detail of your business case proportionate to the scale of investment and the level of risk to your organisation.

Executive summary: key issues and conclusions
Summary of:

✔ Why undertake the project: the issue to resolve or the opportunity available

✔ The outcomes offered by the project

✔ Recommendations of this business case

✔ Headline reasons to justify the recommendations

Rationale

✔ Strategic context

✔ Drivers for change

✔ Goals and objectives

✔ External comparisons

✔ Options

✔ Proposed solution

Analysis

Evaluation of the pros and cons of each option, and value-for-money considerations:

- ✔ Financial and non-financial benefits
- ✔ How to realise and measure the benefits
- ✔ Financial and non-financial costs
- ✔ Affordability and achievability
- ✔ Risks and issues, dependencies and constraints
- ✔ Impact analysis
- ✔ Investment appraisal

Business case approval process

- ✔ How and by whom the business case is to be approved
- ✔ Document control information
- ✔ Approval status

Appendices

Other things that you may want to include:

- ✔ Procurement options and selection
- ✔ Governance and expenditure authorisation processes
- ✔ Relevant policy and strategy papers
- ✔ Cross-reference project definition and planning documents
- ✔ Change control (for the project and for the business case)
- ✔ Business case author and development team
- ✔ The project team

Organising yourself

On the page overleaf is a sample template for a simple business case document. You can download a copy of this and of a fuller version, both of which you can adapt to your own needs, from **www.manageagreatproject.co.uk**

Business case template

Executive summary	• Why undertake the project: the issue to resolve or the opportunity available • The outcomes offered by the project • Recommendations of this business case • Headline reasons to justify the recommendations
Rationale	• Strategic context • Drivers for change • Goals and objectives • External comparisons • Options • Proposed solution
Analysis	Evaluation of the pros and cons of each option, and value-for-money considerations: • Financial and non-financial benefits • How to realise and measure the benefits • Financial and non-financial costs • Affordability and achievability • Risks and issues, dependencies and constraints • Impact analysis • Investment appraisal
Business case approval process	• How and by whom the business case is to be approved • Document control information • Approval status
Appendices	Other things that you may want to include: • Procurement options and selection • Governance and expenditure authorisation processes • Relevant policy and strategy papers • Cross-reference project definition and planning documents • Change control (for the project and for the business case) • Business case author and development team • The project team

Developing your business case

Before you start work on your business case, the most important thing to know is who it is for. When you know who the decision makers are, you can find out what information they need and how they want you to present the information. Whilst many organisations will specify a format for your business case, there will always be room for you to adapt and use that format to meet the preferences of those you need to influence. In gathering and preparing information, consult as widely as you can, to minimise your chances of missing something important. But then apply the *80-20 rule* – a large majority of the total benefit from your project will arise from a small number of big benefits. Build your case on one, two or at most three big arguments. Do not try to list dozens of small reasons to do the project. There are three reasons for this:

1 **Shorter lists of reasons are more persuasive than long lists.** One or two big reasons to do something grab our attention. If the list is long, then by the time we are reading the ninth reason, we have forgotten the first and second. The ninth is probably pretty flimsy, but the weaker reasons dominate our mental assessment.

2 **Focus is a good thing.** In delivering your project, it will be helpful to focus on delivering a few big benefits, rather than dissipate your effort across peripheral ones. If you have promised lots of small benefits, you will have to give them your attention too.

3 **It is in the nature of projects that some of what is promised may not be delivered.** If your business case is so marginal that you need to base it on a whole load of small benefits, your project is likely to under-deliver and be seen as a failure. Declare that now and avoid wasting time and resources on it.

Leave the little additional benefits to other people to raise. Build your case on a few big benefits.

On the other hand, do include all the costs that you are able to identify. Hiding costs now will only reflect badly on you later, when the project is forced to incur them. Better yet, include a generous contingency of extra cost too. If your business case is still compelling, you will be able to feel secure in its robustness.

Documenting the rationale

You can think of this section as falling into two parts: context and solution.

Context

Your business case needs to be a free-standing document and so contain all the information that your decision makers need. So you need to establish the context of your project and the problem or opportunity that it needs to address. Because you will use your business case to evaluate your proposed project, you also need to set up the objectives in addressing the problem or seizing the opportunity – against which you can evaluate options. Finally, you also need to identify and assess any relevant comparisons with other organisations.

> ### What goes wrong?
> Projects often fail because their goal is disconnected from the organisation's other priorities: its organisational mission, vision, values and strategy.

Solution

The second part of your rationale needs to put forward a number of options to solve the problem or take advantage of the opportunity. These will be outline project descriptions that you can compare to show which one has the greatest chance of success or offers the best value for money. A business case may, of course, take forward more than one option, assessing each in detail, but leaving it to your decision makers to make the final evaluation. State clearly which option or options will be subject to a detailed analysis.

Tricks of the trade
SWOT analysis (Strengths, Weaknesses, Opportunities and Threats)

A simple, yet effective way to assess your project options is to use a SWOT analysis. For each option, assume the project has been implemented successfully.

Comparing it to alternatives, what are its relative strengths and weaknesses? Considering the situation you anticipate, what opportunities does it open up, and what threats does it expose?

SWOT ANALYSIS

Evaluating the pros

A benefit is an improvement of some kind. It could have direct measurable effects or intangible, but nonetheless real, consequences; like happiness. The benefit may be quantifiable in financial terms, or it may not – although beware of economists: they will quantify anything in financial terms.

Useful checklist
Typical types of benefits

✔ **Revenue enhancement or acceleration.** The *obvious* one that most businesses focus on.

- ✔ **Cost reduction, cost avoidance or cost control.** The other obvious one, not just for the commercial sector. Reduction of waste is often an easy target to start with.
- ✔ **Enabling benefits.** Establishing infrastructure or processes that pave the way for another project to succeed, which then delivers other benefits.
- ✔ **Mandatory or compliance benefits.** You will be no better off for achieving these benefits, but you will avoid regulatory or legal penalties.
- ✔ **Quality of service.** This may be designed to improve revenue, reduce the cost of complaints or be a valued benefit in itself, resulting purely in greater levels of satisfaction.
- ✔ **Increased productivity.** Similar to cost reduction – but this is the ability to get more with the resources you already have.
- ✔ **Increased motivation.** You may want to get more productivity or better service from your people, or just make them feel better about their work. This can reduce absences and general workplace stress too.
- ✔ **Flexibility.** Setting up the ability to make quick changes in response to sudden events is often a significant benefit.
- ✔ **Management or organisational benefits.** Examples include knowledge sharing, or improved use of skilled resources by creating fairer staff recruitment, development and promotion processes.
- ✔ **Risk reduction.** Whether at an organisational or a lower level, reducing the likelihood or impact of a threat, or simply preparing to handle it if it should manifest, are valuable actions.

Getting the benefits

Your business case should also contain information about how the benefits you have identified will come about. Where, when and how will they accrue, and how will you measure them, to ensure that they have been fully delivered?

There are two types of measure that you can use to evaluate delivery of benefits:

1 **Output and performance measures (OPMs).** These are direct measures of performance or results that are of value. For example, surveys can reveal customer or user satisfaction levels.

How to manage a great project

2 **Performance indicators (PIs).** Where you cannot directly measure the effects that matter, use performance indicators as proxies. Select PIs that you believe relate directly to what you are interested in. The danger is that you will manage to the PI and, if it is poorly chosen, you will not get the results you want. For example, if you cannot measure satisfaction levels, you choose to measure the number of complaints as a proxy. However, a poorly executed complaints procedure makes complaining unappealing, reducing complaints. So inadequate training can reduce both satisfaction and complaints levels together.

Whether you choose to use financial performance measures such as turnover, cost or profit, or non-financial measures like complaints, failure rates or delivery times, one task will be essential – and you may want to include it in your business case: you need to establish a baseline set of data, before your project starts.

Evaluating the cons

The primary costs of doing your project will be … the costs. The financial implications of a project include:

→ **The capital cost of implementation.** Asset purchases like land, buildings, plant and equipment, for example.

→ **The revenue cost of implementation.** Day-to-day costs like staff time (including on-costs of employment, accommodation and equipment, for example), supplies and materials, licence and service fees.

→ **The cost of financing.** If your project needs to borrow money in some way, you need to include the interest charges.

→ **The on-going operational costs.** Once you have delivered the products your project has been set up to produce, there will be costs associated with operating them.

→ **Maintenance costs.** It is good to identify these separately from other operating costs.

→ **Decommissioning costs.** At the end of the life of your product or asset, there may be costs in disposal, or making it safe. This is particularly true for some capital assets.

You would be wise to enlist the help of someone with financial or accounting training to support you in preparing your cost analysis. They will be able to help you to prepare project cash flow statements and balance sheets, if your organisation needs them, or if the scale of your project merits them. As a minimum, you will need to prepare a project budget that sets out all the costs under standard headings.

EXAMPLE PROJECT CASH FLOW STATEMENT

	Year 1	*Year 2*	*Year 3*	*Year 4*
Capital costs 1 2				
Revenue costs 1 2 3 4 5				
Staff costs 1 2 3				
Total cost				

What goes wrong?

Projects fail when there is too much focus on costs, such as the price of contracts, and too little focus on the balance between cost, risk and value.

Organising yourself

On the page opposite is a sample template for a simple project budget. You can download a copy of this, which you can adapt to your own needs, from **www.manageagreatproject.co.uk**

Project budget template

Project capital costs		
1		
2		
3		
4		
Total capital costs		
Project revenue costs		
1		
2		
3		
4		
Staff costs		
Financing costs		
Total project revenue costs		
On-going operational costs		
1		
2		
3		
4		
Maintenance costs		
Total on-going operational costs		
Decommissioning costs		
1		
2		
3		
4		
Total decommissioning costs		
Total projected costs		
Project contingency		
Total project budget		

Assumptions

Alongside your budget and any other financial statement, you must tabulate the assumptions on which your figures are based. The UK Department for Transport famously got into a pickle in 2012, comparing bids to run a rail franchise where they neglected to note the differing assumptions about inflation. Don't make that mistake.

Useful checklist
Typical financial assumptions

There is no right or wrong about what assumption to choose with these. But choose one, apply it consistently and state it clearly.

- ✔ Treatment of future inflation (particularly for longer projects).
- ✔ Treatment of interest rates.
- ✔ Treatment of taxation – such as National Insurance, Capital Gains Tax or VAT.
- ✔ Key numbers that are uncertain at time of preparing your business case – such as staff numbers, revenue figures, or grants.
- ✔ Renewal costs of subscriptions, licences or permits.
- ✔ Maintenance or other service charges.
- ✔ Staff salary costs (real data is rarely available to project teams).
- ✔ Staff on-costs (usually shown as a percentage of salary costs).
- ✔ Consulting or contractor hourly or day rates.
- ✔ Legal and other professional service fees.

Risks, issues and related matters

One of the disadvantages of a project is the risks it incurs. We will examine this in depth in 'Step 6: What if it goes wrong?' Here, it is sufficient to note that your business case must set out the main risks with a brief assessment of the biggest threats. You may also want to include the outline of any contingency plans you have in mind (remembering to include the cost of these in your budget).

In the same section, you can also note any known problems or issues affecting your choice of project, any constraints upon your implementation choices, and any dependencies between your project and other activities within or outside of your organisation.

Tricks of the trade
DCARI

DCARI is a memory aid that stands for Dependencies, Constraints, Assumptions, Risks and Issues.

Weighing the balance

Balancing benefits against costs, pros against cons, can be done both qualitatively and quantitatively.

Qualitative assessment

The simplest approach is a 'for and against' table that is formally known as a *force-field analysis*. You tabulate the pros and cons in two columns and use judgement to assess where the balance lies.

You can make this more structured by rigorously removing any duplication of factors, so that each list contains independent items. The next step is to give each one a weight – say from one to five – representing how significant the factor is. It is best to keep the weighting approach simple. Then you can add up the weights on each side, to get a measure of the balance between pros and cons. If the difference is very small, I would suggest that it is unsafe to rely on the number you generate.

If lots of people follow the same process but make independent judgements, you can gain a lot of insight from the range of the results they get. You can also subject their results to simple statistical analysis. An average will tell you the majority view and you can calculate the standard deviation to tell you if that view is significant.

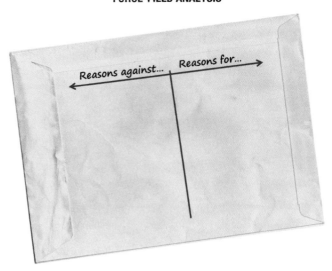

Quantitative assessment

Accountants and finance experts have developed a range of tools of varying sophistication to analyse the financial cost–benefit of an investment – which is what your project would be. The simpler ones take no account of the timing of costs and benefits. The more complex recognise that a payment today is worth more than a payment next year, because inflation erodes the value of money. This is the so-called *time value of money*.

Simple financial assessment tools

Here are three simple tools you can use.

1 The simplest tool of all is a *cost-benefit ledger*. This is the financial equivalent of the force-field analysis, tabulating costs and benefits and comparing them.

COST-BENEFIT LEDGER

Costs		Benefits	
1	£	1	£
2	£	2	£
3	£	3	£
4	£	4	£
Total cost (C)	£	Total value of benefits (B)	£
Net benefit or (cost) = B – C			£

2 From this, you can readily calculate a simple *return on investment* or ROI. This is a percentage figure that allows you to compare the net benefit of a range of different investments. It is calculated as:

$$ROI = 100 \times \frac{\text{(total benefit} - \text{total cost)}}{\text{total cost}} = 100 \times \frac{B - C}{C}$$

3 Another simple yet important measure is the *breakeven period* or *payback time*. We create a simple cash flow (monthly, quarterly or even yearly) and show the following summary lines:

a. Total cost for the period

b. Total benefit for the period

c. Net benefit for the period (= b – a)

d. Cumulative net benefit (the total of the net benefit for this period and all previous periods)

The period in which the net benefit first becomes sustainably positive is the breakeven period. If it becomes positive for a short while and then reverts to negative benefit (cost) this is not true breakeven. The further out from the start your breakeven period is, the higher your risk will be. The table on the next page gives an example of a breakeven cash flow for our greenhouse project.

The greenhouse project

BREAKEVEN CASH FLOW

	Year 1	Year 2	Year 3	Year 4	Year 5
Capital costs 1 Greenhouse	£250				
Revenue costs 1 Labour 2 Fixings 3 Compost 4 Seeds	£100 £50 £50 £20	£20 £20	£20 £20	£50 £20	£20 £20
Total cost for period	£470	£40	£40	£70	£40
Benefits 1 Sale of produce 2 Savings on groceries 3 Health benefits*		£50 £100	£100 £150	£150 £200	£150 £200
Total benefit for period	£0	£150	£250	£350	£350
Net benefit for period	– £470	£110	£210	£280	£310
Cumulative net benefit	– £470	– £360	– £150	+ £130	+ £440

* Not quantifiable

Time-value-based financial assessment tools

Note: many readers will be able to skip this section with no adverse consequences because either you will not need this level of financial sophistication or you will have financially adept colleagues who will be able to do this for you.

The more sophisticated financial assessment tools are based on the time value of money and will need an assumption of how the value of money diminishes year on year. This is called the *discount rate*. At the time of writing (end of 2013), the UK Treasury uses a discount rate of 3.5 per cent, which it has used since 2003.

Let's do a simple example. The cost of our project is £20,000, of which we will spend half this year (year 0) and half next year (year 1). The result will be a cash saving of £5,000 per year, starting in year 2. A simple cash flow and breakeven analysis would look like this:

SIMPLE PROJECT CASH FLOW

Year	A: Cost	B: Benefit	Total (B–A)	Cumulative
0	£10,000		−£10,000	−£10,000
1	£10,000		−£10,000	−£20,000
2		£5,000	£5,000	−£15,000
3		£5,000	£5,000	−£10,000
4		£5,000	£5,000	−£5,000
5		£5,000	£5,000	−
6		£5,000	£5,000	£5,000

Now let's include the time value of money. We need to calculate the *present value* of money spent in the future. To do this, we need to calculate a *discount factor* based on our discount rate (r). We will follow the UK Treasury and use 3.5 per cent. The discount factor is calculated from r and the year (n = 0, 1, 2 ...) using this formula:

$$D[n] = 1 / (1 + r)^n$$

We then calculate the present value of our cost or benefit by multiplying it by the discount factor. Let's take a look (note: all the figures are rounded).

DISCOUNTED PROJECT CASH FLOW

Year	A: Cost	B: Benefit	Total (B–A)	Discount factor (to 2dp)	Present value	Cumulative
0	£10,000		−£10,000	1.00	−£10,000	−£10,000
1	£10,000		−£10,000	0.97	−£9,662	−£19,662
2		£5,000	£5,000	0.93	£4,668	−£14,994
3		£5,000	£5,000	0.90	£4,510	−£10,485
4		£5,000	£5,000	0.87	£4,357	−£6,127
5		£5,000	£5,000	0.84	£4,210	−£1,917
6		£5,000	£5,000	0.81	£4,068	£2,150

The *net present value* or NPV over six years is the sum of all of the present values: in this case, £2,150. Because it is positive, this is a positive investment over a six-year period. We can calculate this over 10, 20 or as many years as we want. Over ten years, the NPV is just over £17,000. We could compare this with the NPVs of other possible projects, to consider which will give us the best return.

Another way of expressing the ROI is to find the discount rate that, over the period in question, would give an NPV of precisely zero. In our example, the NPV at year 6 is £2,150. If we had chosen a discount rate of 6.695 per cent, the NPV at year 6 would have been £0 precisely. 6.695 per cent is called the *internal rate of return* or IRR for this cash flow.

Organising yourself

You can download a spreadsheet discounted cash flow tool (which uses the figures from the previous example), which you can adapt to your own needs, from **www.manageagreatproject.co.uk**

Making the decision

A business case will become one of the most important of your project documents … once it has received formal sign-off. The sign-off is your formal authority to proceed.

The decision process is important. There are three criteria for a sound decision. Since we need to know whether our decisions are sound at the point of making them, none of these three criteria is that the decision is 'right': we can only know that with the benefit of hindsight.

The three criteria are:

1 **Right people.** That the right people, with the correct level of authority and sufficient knowledge, expertise or experience, make the decision.

2 **Best evidence.** That the decision is informed by the best available evidence and analysis. Clearly there is a trade-off between the quality of the data and analysis against the time and resources available.

3 **Sound process.** That the decision follows a sound process that allows decision makers to test and interrogate the evidence and gives time for a range of views to be heard and explored. Before the decision is made, the decision makers should choose the appropriate decision process; for example: unanimity, consensus, majority or a single person's decision, informed by the debate.

Lessons from the real world

1 Do you know why you are doing your project? If you do not, it will probably fail.

2 Present your options appraisal fairly and in an easy-to-assimilate fashion. If you mislead your client [or boss], your actions will just come back and bite you later.

3 If you aren't good with figures, find someone who is. Don't let your business case be undermined by arithmetic or methodological errors.

4 Make sure your project is fully aligned with your organisation's strategy over the timescale of project delivery and integration.

5 Make sure stakeholders sign up – literally – to the elements of the business case that are reliant upon their actions during or after the project. That way, it will be easier to hold them to their commitments later on.

Who cares?

Step 3

Essential practices of Step 3

1 Establish effective governance structures and processes.

2 Identify and analyse your stakeholders.

3 Identify the needs and desires of your stakeholders.

4 Reconcile your stakeholders to the scope of your project.

5 Maintain relationships with your stakeholders through listening and influence.

People matter

Mike's rules

Projects would be easy, if it weren't for the people.

People have ideas, opinions, agenda and foibles that get in the way of the smooth running of a neatly planned project. However, without their opinions and ideas, there is not insight or creativity. People don't make projects easy, but they do make them worthwhile.

The simple answer to 'Who cares about your project?' should be 'A lot of people'. If nobody cares, then there will be no point in doing it. However, we can divide the people who care into three broad groups:

1 Those who will supervise your project, overseeing it and making the big decisions. These people are part of the *governance* of your project.

2 Those who will be interested in your project: what's going on and how it will turn out. These are your *stakeholders*.

3 Those who will get involved in helping out with your project, supporting you in making it happen. These people will make up your project *team*.

In this chapter, we will turn our attention to the first two, returning to your project team at 'Step 5: Who will help?'.

Governance

Governance is the term used for the overall supervision of your project. The word's origins are in a Greek word, meaning to steer, which is still relevant to project management today. Along the way, the word has picked up connotations of directing, controlling, influence, regulation and restraint.

In project management there are two primary governance roles: decision making and oversight. The *decision-making* role ensures that the project does the right things, to serve the needs and purposes for which it was commissioned. *Oversight* makes sure that you and your team do it right: following appropriate procedures, managing properly and delivering what is promised.

The governance arrangements can be as varied as the different organisations that commission projects. But there are two principal approaches, which we can characterise as *individual-led* and *group-led*.

The project sponsor and project board

Where project governance is led primarily by one individual, they will take full responsibility in their organisation for the project. This is often the case in private sector projects, where a senior person either promotes the project from the outset or is given that responsibility. This role is usually referred to as the *project sponsor*. In small projects there may be no need for any further layer of governance and, in small organisations, the owner or leader may act as sponsor and retain complete control over all decisions.

For bigger projects, in bigger organisations, the sponsor may need support in their role. Then, there will be a *project board*, a group of senior people with the breadth of skills and experience to help the sponsor to make wise decisions and oversee progress. Sometimes this group is a pre-existing group, like a senior management team or a group of trustees, for example.

It is the project board that has ultimate authority in the group-led approach to governance. Here decisions are made by the board and the sponsor plays a subsidiary role, more akin to a line manager to the project manager.

The sponsor's role

The sponsor may or may not be accountable for the full governance role of decision making and oversight, but these will certainly form a part of their role. But there is more: as a senior person to the project manager, they should be available to act as their supporter, guide, mentor, coach and adviser. Perhaps most central to the concept of a sponsor, however, is the role of promoting the project within and maybe also outside the organisation. It is the sponsor who will be the conspicuous champion for the project, saying in effect 'I, on behalf of this organisation, say that we need this project.'

Tricks of the trade
Sponsorship in PRINCE2 projects

PRINCE2® (PRojects IN Controlled Environments) is a best practice project management methodology developed by the UK government and mandatory for all UK publicly funded projects. Everything in this book is consistent with PRINCE2, although the terminology differs.

PRINCE2 has the role of *senior responsible owner* or SRO. It describes the SRO as 'the owner of the overall business change that is being supported by the project.' It goes on to say that the SRO 'must take personal responsibility for successful delivery of the project'. On smaller PRINCE2 projects, the SRO may act as *project executive*, taking responsibility for ensuring that the project meets its objectives and delivers the projected benefits. On larger projects, the executive may be a different, less senior person. The executive would chair the project board.

Both SRO and executive roles could be described as project sponsor.

The sponsor is therefore an organisational representative who acts as advocate, decision maker and over seer, and who can use their experience and authority to clear paths through the politics, secure resources and offer guidance.

The board's role

The project board either provides the direction and oversight that good governance demands, or it supports the sponsor in their responsibility to do this. It therefore needs a good mix of skills and experience in its membership. Years of research into the functioning of decision-making groups also suggest that the board should not be too big and that its members should be drawn from as wide a pool of candidates as possible to give it the diversity that leads to wise decisions. Members need to trust one another and be prepared to listen to arguments before forming final opinions. And, of course, the board's decisions can only ever be as good as the information it is supplied with.

Tricks of the trade
Board roles to fill

Whilst it is important to keep the number of members low (five is an ideal number; eight is too many), they must fulfil a range of roles. Some members may take on more than one role and, for some projects, not all roles will be needed. Here are the six usual roles that we find in bigger projects:

1 **Chair** or **facilitator:** usually filled by the sponsor (or executive in PRINCE2 language).

2 **Senior user:** essentially, the customer or client for whom the project is carried out.

3 **Senior supplier:** representing all the external suppliers to the project.

4 **Quality champion:** to ensure that the project delivers the right level of quality.

5 **Finance officer:** to oversee the financial management of the project.

6 **Technical expert:** understands deeply what the project seeks to achieve.

In addition, the project manager and integration manager (if there is one – see the section 'The relationship between the project and the business' below) will usually attend a project board, to contribute to discussions and to hear decisions first hand.

Many of the decisions that the board will need to make or advise on will fundamentally revolve around tensions between time, cost, quality and scope. Users and beneficiaries of the project will normally want as much as they can get in terms of scope, functionality and quality, and they will want it as soon as possible at the least cost. The suppliers will resist all of this, arguing for limits on the scope and quality that will make the project easier and less risky to deliver, while pressing for higher budgets and longer time scales. That is the way of the world.

It is the role of the chair of the board to facilitate discussion to transform this from a potential long-running campaign of argument and dissent into a creative tension. They will enlist the support of experts to help guide them.

Another creative tension potentially lies between the quality champion and the finance officer. But their roles should be about process: establishing and guarding procedures for good quality and financial management. This will free them up to support the sponsor in resolving decisions between the senior user and senior supplier, and overseeing the probity and performance of the project.

Project steering group

An alternative name for a project board is *project steering group*, but let's save the term for something else. This harks back to the Greek origin of our word governance: *kubernas*. It meant steering.

What happens if there are a number of user roles, each of which wants to be represented on the project board? What if there are several suppliers, all of which believe their best interests lie in having a seat at the table? And what if the project is technically complex and demands the knowledge and guidance of a selection of experts? With the possibility of not 5 but 15 project board members, a wise chairperson would want an alternative.

The solution is to set up a user steering group to discuss and agree a position that balances the needs of all users. There can also be a suppliers' steering group mandated to represent the commercial views of all project contractors, consultants and suppliers. And an experts', or technical, steering group to research and deliberate on all the technical issues. If the chair of each of these sat on the project board, this would achieve proper representation, without overloading the board.

The project manager's role

The project manager has day-to-day responsibility for setting up, planning, monitoring, controlling and closing down the project. They are responsible to their sponsor and board, with agreed levels of decision-making authority. They will report their progress at agreed intervals and seek authorisation for the big strategic decisions that are outside their competence or authority.

The relationship between the project and the business

A project delivers something that the organisation needs, to help it achieve benefits in terms of strategic objectives like service, product development, revenue enhancement or cost savings. Very often, the project manager will hand over the deliverables to a service or operational manager who will then be responsible for integrating the new processes, products or assets into the day-to-day operation.

RELATIONSHIP BETWEEN PROJECT AND BUSINESS

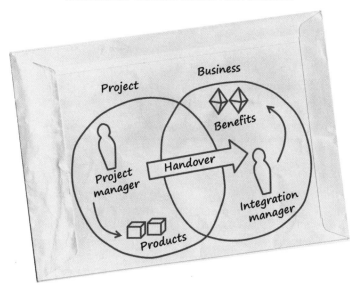

Operational managers have a busy life running their operations; yet integrating something new can require substantial attention and resource. Sometimes, therefore, someone is specifically appointed to manage that process of integrating the new into the current: this is the *integration manager* role. Their concern is to maximise the effectiveness and speed of integration, whilst minimising disruption to the day-to-day processes or services. They will be less focused on the products of the project and more on its outcomes and on realising its benefits.

This generates another creative tension – this time between the project manager and the integration manager. It is at a more tactical level than that between senior supplier and senior user but in the same way, when the roles work well together, they produce the best results for the ultimate beneficiaries of the project.

We can illustrate all the governance roles in one simple diagram:

PROJECT GOVERNANCE ROLES

Useful checklist
Sample role descriptions

Treat these not as prescriptions or a template, but as a starting point for thinking through what is right for your project. Then document your own set of role descriptions.

Project board

✔ Provide overall strategic business direction.

✔ Approve the appointment and responsibilities of the project manager.

✔ Approve key project documents like the definition document (Step 1), business case (Step 2) and plan (Step 4).

✔ Make the key go/no go decisions at stage boundaries, taking account of the strategic fit.

✔ Commit the necessary funds and resources when the project is approved to move from one stage to the next.

✔ Provide the level of project oversight that is consistent with the principles of good governance, and prescribe the format for project reporting to enable this.

✔ Be the point of escalation for any issues arising from the project.

✔ Make decisions within its delegations and identify matters that need to be approved at a higher level. Within this responsibility, dictate requirements on format for requests for decision, respond within agreed timeframe, and set up clear delegation of authority when appropriate.

✔ Act as *change authority*, authorising major changes to specification or the project plan.

✔ Review the lessons learned report and endorse it for circulation, to ensure action.

✔ Approve the end-of-project report and project closure.

Project sponsor

✔ Provide overall strategic business direction to the project.

✔ Identify and brief the project manager.

✔ Provide support, guidance and focus to the project manager when required. ▶

- ✔ Ensure that the scope of the project is fully defined and documented, as well as being consistent with organisational objectives.
- ✔ Conduct project reviews with the project manager to review current status and progress against plans, as well as key project issues, risks and dependencies.
- ✔ Be the point of escalation for any issues or conflicts arising from the project which cannot be resolved by the project manager, and facilitate provision of necessary resources.
- ✔ Make decisions within their delegations and identify matters that need to be approved at higher levels.
- ✔ Provide quality assurance for the project.
- ✔ Represent the project within the department or organisation and outside the organisation.
- ✔ Negotiate solutions at a senior level to problems between the project and external bodies.
- ✔ Chair the project board.

Project manager

- ✔ Understand and document the goal, objectives and scope of the project, and then define the precise scope and specific deliverables required.
- ✔ Deliver key project documentation, such as the project definition document, project plan, business case, and issue and risks logs.
- ✔ Manage stakeholders, listening to their concerns and influencing their actions.
- ✔ Design and develop project plans, stage plans, contingency plans and, where necessary, exception plans to deal with exceptional circumstances.
- ✔ Identify the key people needed for the delivery of the project and bring these people together to form a project team.
- ✔ Allocate tasks to team members and ensure they are completed within the required timeframe and to the required quality.
- ✔ Run regular project team meetings that define the project, plan its delivery, and then review progress and identify required action.
- ✔ Take responsibility for risk and issue management.

- ✔ Manage the day-to-day running of the project, monitoring and controlling performance, taking corrective action when necessary, within delegated authority.
- ✔ Manage the project budget.
- ✔ Produce regular progress reports that show progress against the current plan along with the key project issues, risk and dependencies, and maintain a complete, auditable record of decisions.
- ✔ Liaise with related projects to ensure that work is not overlooked or duplicated, and that resource or schedule interdependencies are managed.
- ✔ Attend project board meetings, providing progress updates.
- ✔ Agree the technical and quality aspects of the project with the appropriate project board members.
- ✔ Complete all actions set out in the project closure checklist (see page 192).
- ✔ Ensure that lessons learned are identified and recorded.

The governance balance

The trickiest aspect of the governance roles that your sponsor and project board have to discharge is balance: telescope view or microscope view? On the one hand, you don't need your bosses taking an acute interest in every detail of your day-to-day project activities. But on the other, you do not want them to take such a hands-off approach that they are neither around to help, nor sufficiently well briefed to spot the problems that you cannot see.

The sponsorship and governance roles are vital to the success of your project, so you must find ways to build relationships and encourage the right level of oversight; one that is able to step back and see the whole project in its context, yet also to zoom in and examine details where necessary. Working at their best, project managers and their sponsors develop an effective working relationship, with the sponsor as your critical friend – able to play both parts, critic and friend, in a way that leaves the relationship enriched, and the project improved.

Stakeholders

A *stakeholder* is anybody who has an interest in your project. They may be affected by its outcome or its process, or they may be able to influence it in some way. The more widely you draw your interpretation of stakeholders, the more control you will have.

Mike's rules

Your stakeholders will determine the success, or not, of your project.

Because of the importance of stakeholders in your project's success, place stakeholder engagement high on your list of priorities. There is a simple, effective, four-stage process for managing stakeholders:

STAKEHOLDER MANAGEMENT PROCESS

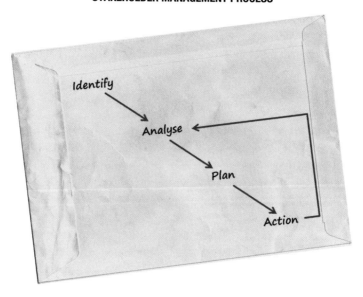

Identify

You cannot do anything until you know who your stakeholders are, so step one is to identify them. The best way to do this is to get a small group of people together to brainstorm every person or group who they can think of, who may have an interest in the project. Don't select just a group of the people you always work with; they will probably all think of much the same set of stakeholders. Include a range of people with different roles, backgrounds and perspectives, to widen the scope of your identification.

A systematic way to identify stakeholders is to think through each item of scope and then ask who may be affected by it, or have an interest in it. Then think through the things you have defined as out of scope: who may have an opinion on those decisions? It is useful for organisations to build up and maintain lists of their stakeholders. These can give project managers a head-start with this process. If there is one, you can draw upon it; if there is not, why not publish your own list and start one today?

Useful checklist
Typical project stakeholders

- ✔ Project sponsor and project board members
- ✔ Users of the service, process or assets you will be creating
- ✔ Your organisation's clients, customers or service users
- ✔ Suppliers and contractors
- ✔ Your project team
- ✔ Colleagues within your organisation
- ✔ Regulators, statutory enforcers and other statutory bodies
- ✔ Directors, business owners, trustees or members
- ✔ Local politicians
- ✔ Accreditation and compliance organisations
- ✔ Banks, insurers and other financial institutions
- ✔ Trade and professional bodies and membership organisations
- ✔ Media (local and national), print, electronic and online social media users
- ✔ Competitors
- ✔ Business and service delivery partners

Analyse

When you know who your stakeholders are, the next step is to understand as much about each of them as you can. At 'Step 1: What do you want?' we considered their attitudes to scope, looking at each stakeholder's needs, wants and preferences. But there is a lot more to understand about them.

What goes wrong?

Projects fail when stakeholders have unrealistic expectations, leading them to determine the project a failure despite it meeting its sponsor's and team's goal and objectives.

A first step in analysis is called *triage* – literally sorting your stakeholders by a small number of particularly salient criteria. A good framework is to start with these two criteria:

1 The extent to which you expect a stakeholder to support or oppose your project.

2 The extent to which each stakeholder's influence can have an impact on your project.

These criteria give you a simple four-box categorisation of your stakeholders (see diagram opposite).

The greenhouse project

Stakeholder analysis:

– Family members	High impact, supportive
– Neighbours	Low impact, opposers
– Local gardening club	Low impact, supportive
– Local builder	High impact, neutral/supportive

Beyond putting them in boxes, however, this choice of criteria leads us to four simple strategies for managing your stakeholders.

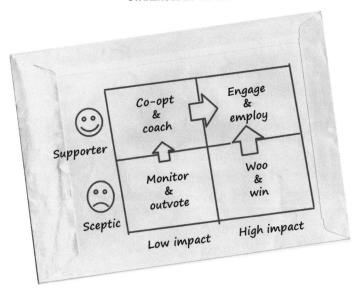

High-impact opposers

These stakeholders don't like what you are doing and have the influence to get in your way, so make it a high priority to either persuade them of the benefits of your project or, at the very least, neutralise their opposition. Your strategy should be to 'woo and win' them: do anything that is legal and ethical to win them around, paying them individual attention, if you need to.

What goes wrong?

Projects fail when people resist the changes that the project brings, or they resist participating in the process – often because their role in the project's success is undervalued.

Low-impact supporters

These stakeholders like what you are doing and may want to help. Unfortunately, you have rated their level of influence as low, so you need to co-opt their active support and then coach them as to how to make that support effective.

High-impact supporters

Your favourite stakeholders will be those who support what you are doing and can be influential with others. Your strategy must be to get them as engaged as possible and then to employ them as advocates for your project.

Low-impact opposers

These sad stakeholders don't like what you are doing but they can't have much impact on you. It is tempting, therefore, to just ignore them. Don't. First, it is not respectful, and second, they may have more influence than you think – or be able to acquire it by joining forces. Instead, inform them and try to persuade them, but manage the project's relationships with them using minimal resources: replace face-to-face meetings with phone calls and emails; replace personal letters with less personal newsletters. Ultimately, your strategy must be to monitor them for possible changes in their level of influence, but to recognise that, because they have little influence, you may have to just accept their opposition and outvote them.

Fence sitters

Some stakeholders are neither opposed nor supportive. They fall into two categories: 'don't know' and 'don't care'. 'Don't care' stakeholders perceive that the project will either have no effect on them or, if it will, there is nothing they can do about it. Pragmatically, there is little of value you can do to manage apathetic stakeholders except to treat them with courtesy and respect. The 'don't know' stakeholders, however, should take high priority. Arguably, they will yield maximum impact for minimum effort, because they need to be persuaded. If you don't work on them, your detractors may, tipping them away from your project. In political terms, these are the undecided 'floating voters'.

Detailed analysis

Putting people into one of four boxes is simple and convenient, but will never reveal the true subtlety of what is, after all, politics. So the second stage of stakeholder analysis is to consider each stakeholder, in priority order, with more care. Consider what you really know about them and use that as a basis for a carefully considered assessment that will form the basis of your plan.

How to manage a great project

Useful checklist
Factors to consider in stakeholder analysis

✔ Ability to influence others
✔ Attitudes
✔ Resources they can deploy to help or frustrate you
✔ Interests/special interests
✔ Needs/special needs
✔ Their commitment to their position
✔ The time they have available to support or oppose
✔ What you want from them and could get from them
✔ How and to what extent they are affected by the project
✔ How to communicate with them
✔ Demographic make-up (of stakeholder groups)
✔ Prior information they've had (and therefore any prejudices they may hold)
✔ Past behaviours and pre-existing relationships with them
✔ Power of their contacts
✔ Level of partisanship/impartiality
✔ Their expectations of your project
✔ Where they are in their organisation
✔ Interdependencies between stakeholders

Organising yourself

On the page overleaf is a sample template for a stakeholder analysis. You can download a copy of this, which you can adapt to your own needs, from **www.manageagreatproject.co.uk**

Plan

Once you have analysed your stakeholders, you need to build a stakeholder communications strategy and a communications plan for each one. The next main section in this chapter examines your communications planning in detail.

Stakeholder analysis template

Stakeholder name/description

Their interest in the project	High ☐	Medium ☐	Low ☐
Their attitude to the project	Negative ☐	Neutral ☐	Positive ☐
Their level of influence	High ☐	Medium ☐	Low ☐
Who they can influence			
The risk they pose to the project	High ☐	Medium ☐	Low ☐
What we want or need from them			
Proposed actions			
Overall priority	High ☐	Medium ☐	Low ☐

How to manage a great project

Action

There is no progress without action. You plans must allocate responsibilities and set timescales. As project manager, you must ensure that the plan is followed and outcomes reviewed.

The four steps (identify, analyse, plan, action) are guaranteed to succeed ... sometimes. To make them really work for you, you need to be persistent. Having taken action, review the results: did you get what you planned to get? If you did: well done. If not, analyse what happened, come up with a new plan, and take more action. This *plan-do-review* loop is the secret to success in much of organisational (and, indeed, personal) life.

Plan your communication

Mike's rules

You can never communicate enough with your stakeholders ... until you hit the point where you have communicated too much.

We want to know what is going on, but there comes a point where we get too much information and feel overwhelmed by it. Unfortunately, the dividing line between the two is vanishingly narrow.

Communication will take up a good half to three-quarters of your time as a project manager – whether it is with team members, customers or clients, bosses or your other stakeholders. If you fail to communicate enough, people will fill the gaps in information with rumours and gossip – which breed mistrust and fear.

Like all skills, getting good at communication requires practice, but the best starting place is a willingness to engage with and care about other people, along with a well thought-out plan.

Mike's rules

The best way to communicate with somebody is the way that they like to communicate.

There are a number of elements in a *stakeholder communication plan*, which will have a section for each stakeholder. Here are the seven core components.

1 **Stakeholder.** The target of your communication.

2 **Message.** The information you need to convey. There may be a series of messages, meaning that you will need a plan for each stakeholder.

3 **Method and medium.** How will you best be able to convey your message? There is a handy checklist of the many forms of project communication you can use, below.

4 **Tone or style.** Are you planning to sell or tell, consult or command, inform or inquire, instruct or inspire, request or require? Setting the tone in advance allows you or a colleague to review the tone of your draft message before it goes out, to avoid miscommunicating by giving the wrong impression.

5 **Timing or frequency.** Determine the best timing for your message or, if you need a cycle of messages, the frequency and timing.

6 **Feedback mechanism.** Have you ever tried to communicate something only to find it has not been understood or, worse, it has been misunderstood? You need to create a way to test the impact your messages have and to get feedback and responses from your stakeholders. One of the most important (arguably, *the* most important) forms of stakeholder communication is listening.

7 **Person or people responsible.** Document who will be responsible for drafting, approving and issuing each message, and then gathering and evaluating feedback.

Useful checklist
Media and tools for communicating your message

You won't want to use all of these, but do select a few, rather than rely on one means of communication for all stakeholders, throughout all stages of your project.

- ✔ Face-to-face, one-to-one (the gold standard)
- ✔ Group meetings, events, conferences
- ✔ Presentations and Q&A sessions

- ✔ Telephone, video conference, text and instant messaging
- ✔ Email (possibly the worst communication method of all – take care)
- ✔ Reports, memos, brochures and other printed documents
- ✔ Websites, blogs and wikis
- ✔ Social media (public or closed systems) like Twitter, LinkedIn, Facebook
- ✔ Project team software
- ✔ Broadcast media (newspapers, magazines, radio, television)
- ✔ In-house media (your organisation's house magazine or newsletter)
- ✔ Videos and audio podcasts
- ✔ Letters
- ✔ Newsletters – print or electronic
- ✔ Posters, signs and notices

Organising yourself

On the page overleaf is a sample template for a stakeholder communication plan. You can download a copy of this, which you can adapt to your own needs, from **www.manageagreatproject.co.uk**

Useful communication skills

As a project manager, you should be constantly learning and acquiring new skills, and honing those you already have. Nowhere is this more so than in the field of communication. It is a huge topic with a lot to say that is relevant for project managers and I have written extensively about many areas. Particular skills you may want to develop, and the books you may want to look at, are:

1 Conversation and presentation – *How to Speak so People Listen*

2 Influence and persuasion – *Brilliant Influence*

3 Negotiation and conflict – *Brilliant Project Leader*

4 Change and resistance – *Handling Resistance Pocketbook*

5 Systematic stakeholder engagement – *The Influence Agenda*

Stakeholder communication plan template

Stakeholder name/description

Objectives

Message to communicate and tone or style	Method and medium of communication	Feedback mechanism – how will we test understanding	Timing and frequency	Person or people responsible
1				
2				
3				
4				

Lessons from the real world

1 Nothing is as logical as you think. The human dimension is all-important. Never leave any assumptions about people untested.

2 Ensure that the right people are overseeing your project and that they are doing it for the right reasons. They must be prepared to take their share of responsibility and not just be there for the kudos.

3 Be sure to document your client's, sponsor's, boss's and board's obligations towards your project.

4 Clients and sponsors only enjoy surprises on birthdays and holidays: never on work days.

5 Be very clear what your project board has decided … and get it in writing.

6 Your stakeholders will see the world differently to you. This does not make them wrong, so stay respectful and listen carefully.

7 Keep your stakeholders up-to-date, unless you want rumours to fill the gaps left by absence of knowledge.

8 What matters most about your communication is how people react to it.

How will you get what you want?

Step 4

Essential practices of Step 4

1 Identify all your deliverables.

2 Set specifications and quality standards for all your deliverables.

3 Establish your timescale and milestones.

4 Create a work breakdown structure (WBS).

5 Create an organisational breakdown structure (OBS), consistent with your WBS.

6 Determine the logical sequence of WBS activities.

7 Estimate the duration of each WBS activity.

8 Create a project schedule.

9 Create a phased project budget, from a bottom-up cost breakdown structure (CBS).

10 Identify and secure all necessary materials, assets and other resources.

The Book of the Plan

When I started out in project management, the first task I was given at the start of a new project was to get a new lever-arch folder from the stationery store and then ask the typing pool to create a front sheet for it. On the front sheet, it had the following information:

→ The project reference number and name.

→ The name of the client.

→ The name of the project manager.

→ The date.

This folder would be known as the *Book of the Plan*. Every element of planning and preparation from briefing notes to budgets would be stored in here. It was our essential reference document for day-to-day management, and our ultimate audit trail of controlled and authorised documents, and due diligence.

Every project needs a Book of the Plan; whether you call it a *project initiation document* (PID), a *project terms of reference* (TOR), a master plan or your project bible. It will contain everything that the team needs to know, to make the project happen. It must therefore answer three questions:

1 What?

2 Why?

3 How? (… and, alongside: When? Where? and Who?)

THE BOOK OF THE PLAN

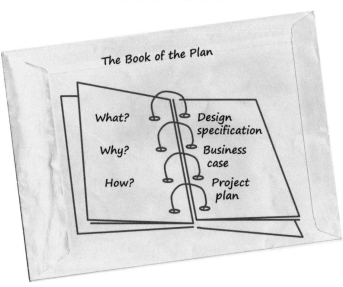

Organising yourself

On the page overleaf is a sample template for your Book of the Plan. You can download a copy, which you can adapt to your own needs, from **www.manageagreatproject.co.uk**

How will you get what you want?

The Book of the Plan template

What?

The project goal and objectives	

The Book of the Plan defines the project. The project definition document forms a part of this and should be reviewed and attached to each revision of the Book of the Plan.

☐ Revised project definition document attached

Indicate which of these attachments are included with the Book of the Plan:

☐ Statement of requirements   ☐ Schedule of deliverables

☐ Quality standards   ☐ Specifications of deliverables

Why?

The reasons for undertaking the project	

Indicate which of these attachments are included with the Book of the Plan:

☐ Business case   ☐ Benefits statement

☐ Project budget   ☐ Benefits realisation plan

How?

Approach to delivering the project	
Project organisation	
Project acceptance criteria	

Indicate which of these attachments are included with the Book of the Plan:

☐ Project plan   ☐ Work breakdown structure

☐ Quality plan   ☐ Resource plan

☐ Risk log   ☐ Equality impact assessment

☐ Communications plan   ☐ Health and safety plan

How to manage a great project

What?

The *What?* question will be answered by a full list of the deliverables that your project will produce, along with detailed specifications and quality standards for each one. This was our focus at Step 1. In the Definition stage of your project, you will usually be satisfied with a list of the deliverables (or maybe just the major ones) and references to essential quality standards and functional requirements.

By the end of the Planning stage, you will need a detailed specification of every deliverable, which is signed off by your client. That way, at the end of the Delivery stage, your client, boss or customer can compare what you have delivered against your agreed specification and formally accept handover. If there is no detailed definition of what the finished project must look like, then you are doomed to discussions, arguments and recriminations, when your deliverables do not match your client's expectations.

Why?

The *Why?* question is answered by your business case, which compares your project's costs and benefits. We examined this fully at Step 2. In the Definition stage of your project, this will take the form of broad cost estimates and an outline statement of benefits, sufficient to show that it is worth investing more time and effort in defining and planning your project fully. By the end of the Planning stage, you will have detailed specifications and plans to base your benefit and cost estimates on, so you will have a full business case that can act as the basis of a considered investment decision.

How?

The *How?* question is answered by two things: your plans and your controls. Your plans describe how you will deliver the products you specified and the benefits set out in your business case, and your controls will show how you will stick to your plans or, if things go wrong, how you will manage the process of getting back on plan, or building a new one.

Step 4 – this chapter – and Step 5 are about your plans and how to create them. Step 4 focuses on the physical elements of your plan:

time, activities, sequence, schedule, budget and material resources. Step 5 then picks up with the human aspects of your plan: enlisting and managing the support of a team of people to help you deliver your plan.

What goes wrong?

Projects fail when plans lack a sound basis for estimates of schedule and resources, leading to unrealistic deadlines and budgets.

We will turn our attention to project controls in Steps 6 and 7. You will find a fuller list there, but the principal project controls are:

→ stage boundaries ('How managing a great project works' – see page 10)

→ risk and issue management (Step 6)

→ schedule control (Step 7)

→ budget management and cost control (Step 7)

→ project reporting (Step 7)

→ change control (Step 7).

Back to Step 4 … Let's work through the process of building a plan. Our first task will be to:

Determine key points along the way

There are two places to start your planning: the timing of your project and what it will deliver. One may well loom larger over you, so pick that one to start with, but which you do first does not really matter, because you will do the other next. So we will start with the timing.

Many people consider the timescale by starting with now and thinking about the key points along the way: 'First we will need to get to here, then to here …' all the way to the end of the project. This is wholly logical, as is the principal alternative: to start at the end and work backwards. So some people will think: 'Before we finish, we need to get to there, and before we get there, we'll need to get here …'. Do you plan forwards or backwards? Each is as good and you'll most often plan backwards when you are given a fixed deadline to meet for delivery of your project. Of course, some of us (yup, including me) have brains like scrambled egg. We don't plan in a logical order, but think of all of the key points randomly, and then sort out the sequence. If that sounds a bit like you, then sticky notes and an empty wall will be a valuable project asset.

Type 1 milestones: Key points

However you identify your key points along the way, they will give you the backbone of your project and are known as *milestones*. Milestones mark the completion of something worthwhile, the commencement of something big, or a decision point. They are a moment in time when something important happens.

Mike's rules

Milestones are your best friends.

For many small projects, a list of milestones, with their dates, is all that you need to plan your schedule. This might be no more sophisticated than a table drawn in your notebook.

The greenhouse project

MILESTONES

No.	Milestone event	Responsible	Date
1	Greenhouse selected and ordered	AJ, BK	31 October
2	Site selected and marked out	BK	14 November
3	Sand, cement, paving and mixer delivered	CL	21 November
4	Path and foundation slab laid	BK	28 November
5	Greenhouse delivered to site	DM	16 January
6	Greenhouse fully assembled	BK	30 January
7	Work surfaces and shelves installed	BK	6 February
8	First planting	BK, EN	20 February

How will you get what you want?

Milestone tables can be used not only for planning your project, but can be extended to give a valuable tool for recording and reporting on progress.

MILESTONE TABLE (STATUS)

No.	Milestone event	Who	Planned date	Forecast date	Actual date	Comments
1						
2						

Organising yourself

You can download a blank milestone table, which you can adapt to your own needs, from **www.manageagreatproject.co.uk**

For people who prefer a graphical representation, there is a simple way to illustrate a milestone plan and subsequently show status:

MILESTONE CHART (TIMELINE)

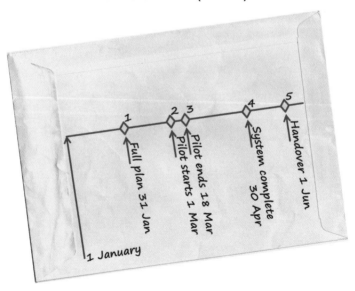

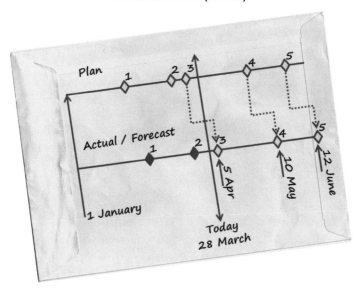

Type 2 milestones: Progress indicators

The metaphor of a milestone is well chosen. Milestones mark important points along a route, but you will also find them at less significant points along the way. These mark progress, and project managers use milestones in this way too.

Suppose you allocate a three-week task to a colleague. Now consider what happens when you ask them, half-way through, how they are getting on: It's going fine,' they say; 'Don't worry.' So, of course, you start to worry. If you and they had agreed, at the outset, what should be achieved by this half-way point, that would have created a milestone: a leading indicator of progress, that you can use to assess whether they are on track, or not.

And the most important thing about a milestone is that it is a moment in time, when something has happened. So milestones are binary: they have either happened or they have not. They therefore give you, unambiguously, a fact. The 'rule' earlier in this section, 'Milestones are your best friends' is true because, like your best friends, milestones will never lie to you. It has either been done, or it hasn't. And if it hasn't, you can enquire into how late it will be and take appropriate action.

If I am late with delivering a type 2 milestone early on in a piece of work, you have a lot of choices. And choice gives you control. You could give me some advice, lend a hand, get someone else to help, split the job with someone else, take the job away from me and give it to someone else, reschedule the job, or reschedule other work around it. If, however, you do not have clear visibility of the delay until close to scheduled completion, then your choices are limited and you have lost control.

Use as many type 2 milestones as you need to feel that you are in control. The less confident you are in my abilities or commitment, and the more critical, complex or uncertain the task is; the more progress indicators you need.

Break down your work into chunks

Projects involve a number of activities that need to be organised and co-ordinated. Perhaps the grand-daddy of project planning tools is the one designed to bring order and structure to all these activities. It is fundamental to the planning and understanding of all complex projects and yet it is under-loved and under-used by many project managers, including some who would describe themselves as professionals in the field. It is called a *work breakdown structure* or WBS.

Work breakdown structure

The name might sound intimidating, but all that a work breakdown structure does is to take the work (your project) and break it down into a structured set of tasks. Let's take an example: redecorating your kitchen.

First: Work streams

Determine the big areas of work in redecorating your kitchen. You might decide that they are: stripping out the old kitchen, electrical work, plumbing, decoration and construction of kitchen units and cupboards.

Second: Key jobs

For each of the work streams, list out what the key jobs will be. For example, in stripping out the old kitchen, you may need to: remove the old cupboards, take up the flooring and strip the walls. You may split the electrical work into the ring main, the lighting circuit and radial circuits for high consumption devices like the cooker.

Third: Detailed work items

For each key job, break it into the detailed pieces of work. One key job of the decorating work stream may be the walls. Detailed work items may be preparation and painting. You may further split each of these down to another level of detail, for example splitting preparation into washing, filling and smoothing.

WORK BREAKDOWN STRUCTURE

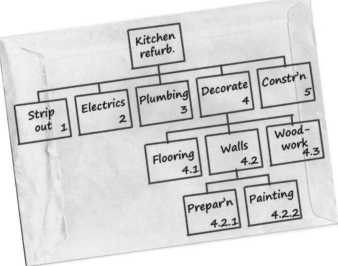

How much detail?

The answer to this question depends largely on who will be doing the work. In general, go down to a sufficient level of detail so that the person or people who will do the work see the work as a single task.

An experienced decorator will read 'preparation' and know exactly what to do. A junior colleague, doing the work for the first time, will need a reminder of the necessary components. The other reason for going into more detail will be to get more precision in other aspects of the planning, which we will cover later, such as budgeting, resource planning or scheduling.

Bottom-up or top-down?

The logic of formal project management requires that you develop your WBS 'top-down' – starting with the project and breaking it into successively finer details. For many of us, working on lower complexity projects in less formal environments, an alternative approach is equally valid and will suit some people better. This is 'bottom-up' and works well when planning collaboratively. Here, you start by listing everything that needs to be done. Then, you cluster similar tasks into groups, and cluster the groups into work streams. This approach is less rigorous, but the lack of formality will make some people more comfortable. A team working together on a WBS will almost certainly adopt some form of hybrid approach.

Tricks of the trade
A MECE WBS

The goal of creating a good WBS is to make it *MECE*, which stands for Mutually Exclusive and Completely Exhaustive.

→ **Mutually exclusive.** Each item appears uniquely – once and once only. Since we will go on to use our WBS as the basis for resourcing, budgeting and scheduling our plan, if something appears twice, it will attract double the resources, be over-budgeted and possibly get done twice.

→ **Completely exhaustive.** Everything that needs to be done is there, on your WBS, somewhere. If it is not, it will get missed from the budget, will not attract the resources it needs and it won't get done. This is sometimes known as the *100 per cent rule*.

Top tip: The commonest things that project managers miss out of their WBS are the activities directly related to managing their project. They then wonder why they have neither the time nor resources to properly manage the work and thus spend their time running around without the time to stop and think.

Four tactics for ensuring MECE

1 **Logic.** A top-down, rigorous approach to creating your WBS is the best way to make sure you miss nothing. Overlaps and duplications are, however, still possible, because one task may logically fit in two different places, depending on your preferences. Deal with each one on its own merits.

2 **Teamwork.** A team working together can harness diversity and dissent to generate creative insights and critical scrutiny. It is also a great way to familiarise your new project team with what needs to get done.

3 **Redo.** There is nothing quite like reviewing something from cold to spot the problems. When you have finished your WBS, lock it in a drawer for a week and forget it. Then get it out and review it. Better still, don't get it out, leave it there and do it again; but this time do it a different way: if you did it top-down, try brainstorming and do it bottom-up. If you did it with a group, work alone. When you have your new WBS, compare the two carefully: what do you learn?

4 **Review.** When you have finished your WBS, give it to the sharpest people you know, who did not get involved in developing it, and ask them to critique it ruthlessly. Take their findings as a gift, not a curse.

WBS and scope

Your resulting WBS is a structured representation of the work before you. The bottom tier is a complete articulation of your scope, so the WBS is the tool we use to articulate scope formally, meeting the promise made at Step 1.

The image of scope as a hierarchical tree diagram, as above, is helpful in understanding it, but becomes unwieldy for real projects. A numbering system, however, allows us represent it as a structured list:

The greenhouse project

Example of a partial WBS:

1. *Procurement*
    1.1. Greenhouse
        1.1.1. Research requirements
        1.1.2. Research selection
        1.1.3. Research best price
        1.1.4. Order
    1.2. Foundation slab
    1.3. Pathway
2. *Ground work*
    2.1. Foundation slab
        2.1.1. Clearance of site
        2.1.2. Digging and levelling
        2.1.3. Pouring concrete
    2.2. Path way
3. *Construction of greenhouse*
    3.1. Frame
    3.2. Securing to slab
    3.3. Glazing
4. *Fit-out of greenhouse*
    4.1. Work surfaces
    4.2. Shelving
    4.3. Ventilation

Organisational breakdown structure (OBS)

Allocate people to each task on your WBS to create an *organisational breakdown structure*, or OBS. The people responsible for work streams are usually referred to as *work stream leaders*. A smaller chunk, or package, of work is referred to as a *work package*, and the person responsible is the *work package manager*.

ORGANISATIONAL BREAKDOWN STRUCTURE

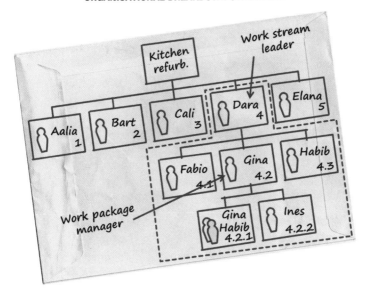

A great way to run a large project, from planning onwards, is to identify and brief talented and capable work stream leaders. You can leave them to devise the WBS elements in their work stream, and to make the necessary cost, resource, time and scheduling estimates, and devote your time to reviewing their work and ensuring co-ordination between the work stream leaders.

Cost breakdown structure (CBS)

Once you have a WBS, the easiest way to generate a budget for your project is to estimate costs for each of the bottom tier of WBS activities. This will include estimates for:

→ Staff and contractor time. (This may require you to make time estimates. We shall return to that topic and, indeed, to estimating in general, later in this chapter.)

→ Accommodation costs or staff on-costs.

→ Equipment or asset hire or purchase.

→ Materials and consumables.

You can then add up items to get costs for each work stream and for the full project. This gives you a *cost breakdown structure*, or CBS. If you already have an OBS, you can allocate budget responsibility at whatever level of the CBS you choose. You may keep all responsibility to yourself, right at the top, or delegate to work stream leaders, or further down to work package managers. You could even choose to allocate responsibility on a task-by-task basis, though I would not recommend that.

You can also add contingency to your budget. There are three approaches:

1 **Top-down.** This is a single contingency sum added to the final budget cost – simple but imprecise.

2 **Bottom-up.** Add a contingency sum to each budget figure and carry the sums up, to give a final contingency for the project. This is precise, but a lot of work. The extreme precision may give false comfort, too.

3 **Hybrid.** Choose an intermediate level – often that of work streams – and apply a single contingency to each item at that level. This recognises that different areas of work have differing levels of uncertainty, and so merit a different level of contingency, whilst it avoids over-precision. I suggest you allocate contingency at the same level as you allocate budget responsibility (or maybe one level above it).

Product and deliverables breakdown structures (PBS and DBS)

In the USA, where scope is more often thought of in terms of the products the project will deliver, the WBS is a structured breakdown of the final deliverables, into their component parts. In the UK, we are more likely to call this a *product breakdown structure*, or PBS.

However, if a WBS is your primary tool for understanding the work, then there is a modified version of the PBS that I recommend, for linking your deliverables to your WBS, and I will call this a *deliverables breakdown structure*, or DBS, to distinguish it.

How to manage a great project

Here, you identify any deliverables that flow directly from each action. If a deliverable flows from a series of actions, attach it to last in the sequence. More than one deliverable could attach to a single task.

DELIVERABLES BREAKDOWN STRUCTURE

Materials and risk breakdown structures (MBS and RBS)

Oh, we could go on and on. Your original WBS can sire a whole army of useful tools. Use your imagination and create the breakdowns that are useful to you and your project. Two that I have used (on one occasion each) are:

1 **Materials breakdown structure:** to add materials requirements to the bottom of my WBS. This allowed us to collate a shopping list to ensure that we ordered all the stock we would need for the project.

2 **Risk breakdown structure:** to identify and reference, rigorously, the risks identified with every project activity.

These are just two examples of the tools you can conceive and turn to useful service, if you need them.

Arrange the chunks into a sequence

A WBS is a useful asset, but it is not yet a plan. This requires at least three more pieces of information for each activity:

1 **The logical sequence of tasks:** usually expressed in terms of the tasks that must come before (predecessors) and after (successors) each task.

2 **The amount of effort or work required to complete the activity:** usually expressed in person-hours or person-days.

3 **The amount of resources (people) allocated to the task:** usually expressed in full-time equivalents or FTEs.

When you put 2, the effort, and 3, the resources, together, this gives you the duration of the task.

The logical sequence gives you the flow of work, from one task to another. When you add the durations, you can calculate when each activity will start and finish.

Estimating

Estimating is one of those challenges that project managers must rise to. An estimate is an assumption of how long something will take or how much it will cost. A good estimate must be accompanied by some indication of the level of confidence that goes with it. In the real world, we know that there is a range of times that an activity could take; for example, from 20 days to 40 days. There may or may not be an absolute minimum, but there will certainly be a best reasonable case. And whilst it could always run into highly unexpected troubles, let's say that 40 days is already unlikely. The figure opposite illustrates the statistical nature of this estimate.

Now, what do we take as the most useful estimate? The most likely figure (26 days), the figure that is equally likely to be too big or too small (28 days), half-way between the highest and lowest estimates (30 days), or the one that you are 90 per cent confident can be achieved (34 days)? None of these is any more 'correct' than the others.

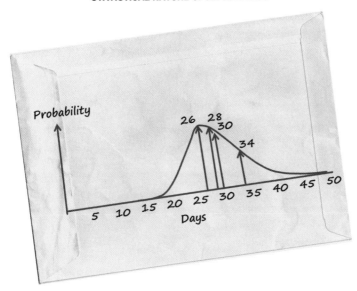

This indicates what a complex subject estimating is. So let's focus on the tips and techniques that pragmatic project managers use in all but the most sophisticated and sensitive project environments.

Tricks of the trade

Estimating

1 Get under the skin of each activity, to really understand it, before estimating either cost or duration.

2 Nothing beats data: look for records of similar projects.

3 If you do not have experience of the activities you are estimating, look for someone who does.

4 Look for reliable 'rules of thumb' that are used for this type of project in your type of organisation.

5 Several independent estimates will vary widely, but the average may be a sound estimate. So, ask lots of people to make their own estimates, and then combine them.

▶

6   Independent estimators should be free to use different techniques if they choose.

7   Always give a confidence level and limits – for example '28 days (–5/+6) to 90 per cent confidence' indicates your estimate is 28 days and you are 90 per cent confident it will not be less than 23 days or more than 34 days.

8   Maybe keep it simple with a best estimate and a contingency – for example 28 (+6) days. A contingency of 10–35 per cent is normal, depending on the uncertainty and your attitude to risk.

9   'Time is money', so a contingency in one demands a contingency in the other.

10 Check your results: do they seem reasonable and is your arithmetic correct?

Useful checklist
Ten common estimating mistakes

✔ Under-allowing for the time and cost of testing, fault-finding, fixing and re-testing.

✔ Submitting to political pressures to adjust estimates, against your better judgement.

✔ Neglecting the cost and time associated with maintenance of tools and equipment.

✔ Forgetting the time people spend in meetings, and other management and admin time.

✔ Not allowing for scope creep.

✔ Not taking account of the effects of complexity on the scale of your task.

✔ Forgetting that team familiarisation takes time and so does the process of collaborating.

✔ Forgetting that your project will have to integrate with other existing and new assets and processes.

✔ Assuming that we can do things more quickly than anyone else. We are rarely correct.

✔ Not allowing for interruptions, distractions, delays, hitches, snags and the myriad other reasons why nothing ever goes as planned.

… Oh yes, and believing your arithmetic. Check and check again!

Network charts

A *network chart* is a way to illustrate the logical sequence of events, like the example below:

NETWORK CHART

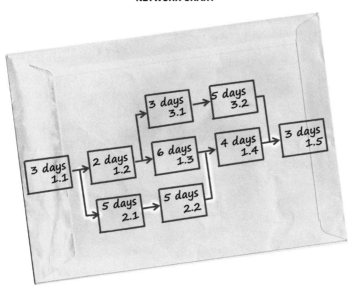

In this figure, the connections from one activity to another are called *dependencies*. Strictly speaking, they are *finish-to-start dependencies*, because the finish of one activity links to the start of the next. We can describe activity 1.3 as 'dependent' on activity 1.2, or as its *successor*. Activity 1.2 is the *predecessor* of 1.3. If we need to wait two hours for the walls to dry, between activities 1.2 and 1.3, we describe this as a finish-to-start dependency with a two-hour *lag*.

As soon as you add the durations on to your network, you can start to calculate schedules. The longest route through your network is called the *critical path* and represents the duration of your project. It is 'critical' in the sense that these are the activities that carry the risk of delay – if any of these activities were delayed, your whole project would miss its deadline.

Look at activities 1.2 and 1.3. These are happening in parallel with activities 2.1 and 2.2, so their duration does not contribute to the critical path. They could slip by up to two days without delaying your project, and these two days are known as *float* or sometimes, more colloquially, as *slack*.

Tricks of the trade
CPM and PERT

The *critical path method* (CPM) was developed by DuPont in the 1950s to help plan research and development projects. It uses network diagrams and calculates critical paths to help schedule and control projects. At around the same time, the US Navy developed the *program evaluation and review technique* (PERT) for the same purpose and the two look very similar. The main difference is that CPM uses a single estimate for each duration while PERT uses a three-point estimate, allowing the whole project schedule to reflect the uncertainty in estimating.

In PERT, the time allocated to a task, the *expected time* (T) is calculated from three times, which we will illustrate using the example from the earlier section on estimating:

1   The most likely time (M) = 26 days.

2   The most optimistic reasonable time (O) = 20 days.

3   The most pessimistic reasonable time (P) = 40 days.

There are two ways that T is commonly calculated, both taking a weighted average of these three numbers M, O and P. The weightings differ, and the more common approach is:

$$T = [(O + (4 \times M) + P)] / 6 = [20 + (4 \times 26) + 40)] / 6 = 27$$

If you want a more pessimistic figure, this formula is also used:

$$T = [O + (3 \times M) + (2 \times P)] / 6 = [20 + (3 \times 26) + (2 \times 40)] / 6 = 30$$

Schedule the chunks of work

Most people find it easier to read a schedule on a chart that explicitly shows time. And the chart we use for this is something of a poster-child for project management: The *Gantt chart*. A Gantt chart represents each activity from your WBS as a bar. The length of the bar represents the duration of the task and its positioning on the chart reflects when it is scheduled – either as a result of the logic of the network or of a scheduling decision made by the project manager. The figure below shows the same plan as the network chart above, in Gantt chart format.

GANTT CHART

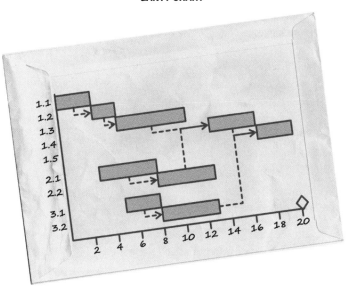

Note that it only takes a cursory examination to read off the duration of the project, and that the two days' float is readily seen. The diagonal bands of activities are what we called work streams, and we have added a milestone marker at the end of the chart.

This chart shows pretty much all of the features of a full-size project Gantt chart. Where additional symbols are used, I would expect a key to make their meanings clear. Sometimes you will see the arrows that indicate dependencies, as here; sometimes they are omitted for clarity. The critical path can be highlighted or not.

Gantt charts can also be used to illustrate progress. In the example overleaf, the vertical line represents 'now' and the bars are shaded to indicate level of progress. Activities that are ahead or behind schedule are therefore easy to identify.

PROGRESS ON A GANTT CHART

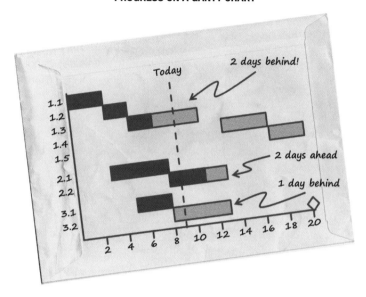

Scheduling choices

Where a task is not dependent on another, you can schedule it to start, or to finish, whenever you choose. The two principal choices are:

→ Finish as late as possible.

→ Start as early as possible.

Often the choice will depend on your attitude to risk and the availability of resources or materials that the tasks need.

Schedule contingency

As you already know, it is vital to put contingency in your schedule. As with the budget contingency, you could work top-down and add a contingency period on to your planned completion date. This is often a red rag to your stakeholder bulls and I do not recommend it. You could instead add a little contingency to each of your activities. The trouble with this is Parkinson's Law:

'Work expands to fill the time available.'

(Cyril Northcote Parkinson, 1955)

If your team members know that they have 15 days, plus three days' contingency, then mentally, they are working to an 18-day deadline. In reality, I would expect much of your contingency to be used up, activity by activity, and I do not recommend this approach. If something unexpected happens, it leaves you with nothing up your sleeve.

You need control of *your* contingency. So, after a series of tasks, schedule an additional dummy task, which will hold all of your contingency. This is yours to control. When your project plan has these contingency periods scheduled between chains of tasks, you will substantially reduce your schedule risk.

These contingencies act like firebreaks. They are *islands of stability* in your schedule that contain the contagion of slippage, allowing you to start subsequent streams of work afresh, and on time. This is one of your most powerful control tools.

ISLANDS OF STABILITY ON A GANTT CHART

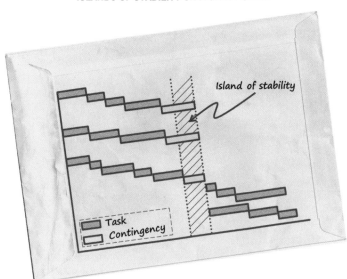

Tricks of the trade
Negotiating contingency

As soon as you try to negotiate any contingency in your schedule (or, indeed, in your budget), stakeholders will resist, wanting to see delivery of your project as soon (and as cheaply) as possible. Here is a handy two-stage technique for mitigating this effect.

Stage 1: Define your negotiating contingency

Start with the estimate you want to use as the basis for your planning, and add to that a *prudent contingency*. Now calculate an additional *negotiating contingency*. Label the total estimate plus all contingency as *planned duration*.

TWO LEVELS OF CONTINGENCY

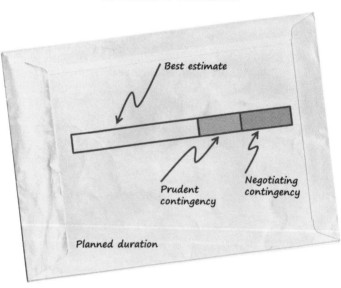

Best estimate

Prudent contingency

Negotiating contingency

Planned duration

Stage 2: Negotiate your contingency

Your first offer should be to halve your negotiating contingency. Subsequent offers should be no more than half of your remaining negotiating contingency. This ensures that you never dip below the level of your prudent contingency.

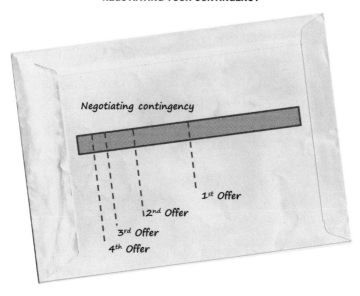

Drawing tools

What can you use to draw your Gantt charts, your network charts and a myriad of other project tools? The first generation of drawing tools – as used by project planners up to the late 1950s – is still valuable today: pencil, paper and ruler. This has the merit of being intimate and showing up mistakes and changes, which encourage others to critique your planning logic freely. Of course, you can produce nicer images using simple software tools like spreadsheet and drawing tools. These are not made for the job, but can do it pretty well.

But if you are serious about project management and have sizeable projects to lead, then you and your team will need access to a purpose-made project planning software tool. There are many on the market and some that are freely available – particularly cloud-based software when used by small teams. Define your needs clearly, research the available tools well, and make the time to learn how to use the software properly – and not as another drawing tool. Remember:

Mike's rules

Software does what you tell it to: not what you want it to.

And no amount of high-quality software will do your job for you. It is you who needs to understand your project, think the plan through, research it, and validate the logic.

Mike's mum's rules

A fool with a tool ... is still a fool.

Resourcing your Gantt chart

We will talk at Step 5 about planning the resources for your project, but it is worth noting that you will need to allocate people to do each of the tasks in your Gantt chart. If you have already done an OBS, this will be easy. The next thing to do is to consider how long the task will take. Tasks fall mostly into two types:

→ **Type 1: Independent of effort.** Some things take as long as they take, regardless of how much work you put in – the arrival of a delivery, for example.

→ **Type 2: Effort-driven.** Some things require a fixed amount of work – usually measured in hours or days.

How long will it take?

For effort-driven work, the duration depends upon the availability of the people who will work on it. If a task takes six days of work, and you have somebody available full time, the effort will be six days, and the duration will be six days. If you have two people able to work full time, the effort will be six days, and the duration will be three days. If you one person able to work half time, the effort will be six days, and the duration will be twelve days.

Identify what you need to do the job

Project managers view people as resources, but they are not the only resources you will need. The next thing to think about is what materials you will need to do the job. This usually splits into consumables and assets.

The greenhouse project

Consumables:
→ frame, glass, fixings

→ sand, cement

→ varnishes, sealants

Assets:
→ mini digger

→ cement mixer

→ assorted hand tools

→ safety equipment – gloves, helmet

The best way to calculate what you need, and the quantities, is to start from your work breakdown structure and create a list for each type of material.

Planning for quality

In Step 1, we saw that there are three processes for getting quality right: quality design, quality assurance and quality control. Crudely, these happen before, during and after the Delivery stage: we design our products to the right quality standards, follow sound processes to deliver them to those standards, and then evaluate the quality of what we have delivered.

How will you be sure to deliver to the quality standards that you specified at Step 1? When you develop your answers to this question, you can use a *quality plan* to document those answers.

Quality plan template

Definition stage: Supporting project definition document

Quality expectations	Set out clearly the agreed level of quality the customer (external and internal users or beneficiaries) can expect, so that the project deliverables meet their required purpose.
Quality criteria	Set out the criteria by which project success and quality will be assessed. List these in order of priority, so that they can inform decisions on priorities. Examples of relevant criteria include: delivery to time, delivery to cost, productivity, functional requirements, customer requirements, performance, user-friendliness, maintainability, security and control, or service level agreement.

Planning stage: Supporting project plan

Quality standards	What quality standards apply to this project? These may include technology, building or management quality standards. These should be fully reflected in any project design documents. **Responsible person:**
Quality assurance	How will the design standards be assured during project implementation? What quality management process will be applied? **Responsible person:**
Quality control	What are the quality control and audit processes that will monitor project deliverables? What review points or review cycle will be used? What elements of the project will be reviewed at each review? **Responsible person:**
Change control	What process will be used to manage and control change, once the delivery phase begins? **Responsible person:**
Responsibilities	Who will take overall responsibility for the quality of the outcomes? Who will review the quality? Who will conduct periodic project reviews, if appropriate? What are the responsibilities of individual project members, with respect to quality?

Organising yourself

On the page opposite is a sample template for your quality plan. It sets out some of the things you will need to consider. You can download a copy, which you can adapt to your own needs, from **www.manageagreatproject.co.uk**

Lessons from the real world

1   Things always take longer than we expect and cost more than budgeted. The problem is that we too often believe our plans. Treat your plan as no more than a first draft. It is not what will happen, just a guide to what might happen.

2   We usually plan based on the actions we expect to take. It is the actions of others that often disrupt our plans. Part of your planning must take account of other people's and organisations' concerns and how they may act as a result.

3   Make sure you are clear about the detail of your cost and schedule estimates. Where do they come from and in what ways can they be wrong?

4   Developing a WBS with your team is a great way to create a shared understanding of what you need to do.

5   Always put enough contingency in your plan so you can watch with equanimity when some of it gets negotiated away.

6   Subject your plans to a *red team review*. Get the smartest, most critical people you can find to scrutinise it and try to pick it apart. You will not enjoy the experience, but neither will you regret it.

7   Never respond to a question with an off-the-cuff estimate of budget, resource needs or schedule. Always take time to give a considered response.

Who will help?

Step 5

Essential practices of Step 5

1 Define project organisation structures.

2 Identify available resources.

3 Define roles and assign responsibilities.

4 Identify workload commitments and reconcile to project schedule and allocation.

5 Create a productive working culture.

Why you need help

Many of us start our project management working on small projects which we manage and carry out entirely on our own: we are project manager, project team and project cheerleader all in one. As the projects you manage grow, there will come a stage where you alone are not enough to get the job done.

There are two reasons why you may need to add further people to the project:

1 Capacity. You may simply need more hours in the day to get things done. Project team members provide intelligent bodies to work on your project.

2 Capability. Project managers like to think of themselves as the all-capable Swiss Army knives of the management arena. Yet there are things you cannot do and team members bring in extra specialisms, skills, knowledge and experience to supplement your own.

Step 5 is therefore about how to introduce, manage and lead the team members who will help you plan and deliver your project.

Planning your support

We have already seen (at Step 4) how your organisational breakdown structure (OBS) is the basis for allocating people to tasks in your project, and then to scheduling their contributions. But how do you select your team members – assuming that is, you get a choice – and how do you choose what roles to put them in?

Start with a simple capability assessment. For each work stream, list the skills your project will need, using a table like this:

SKILLS REQUIREMENT

Skill required	Level required (L, M, H)	Time required	Notes

As well as unskilled team members, who will contribute the breadth of their general experience, their enthusiasm, and their common sense, there are three levels of skill, which correspond to those that skilled trades have recognised since the Middle Ages:

Low: *Apprentice* — Some skills. Able to work effectively with supervision. Typically up to three years' continuous experience.

Medium: *Journeyman* — Fully skilled. Able to supervise one or two apprentice-level team members. Able to work unsupervised, or with minimum supervision. Typically between three and seven years' experience.

High: *Master* — Highly skilled expert. Able to supervise a large team. Able to innovate and resolve the most complex problems. Typically at least seven years' experience.

Organising yourself

You can download a blank skills requirement schedule, which you can adapt to your own needs, from **www.manageagreatproject.co.uk**

If you are unable to start off with a blank sheet of paper in choosing team members, you will have to deploy the team you have available, as best you can. A SWOT analysis can be a great help to you. You read about this in Step 2. Here, you can assess the strengths and weaknesses of each candidate, and look at the opportunities and threats that they offer to your project.

Resourcing challenges

Three challenges frequently face a project manager who wants to get the best people on their team: availability, conflicting commitments and balancing of workloads.

Availability

It often happens that the people we most want on our project teams are unavailable: the things that make them attractive team members to you will also make them attractive to other people. Consequently, project managers often have to manage with the people who are available to them. This puts a premium on your ability to motivate and develop your people, so we will return to this later in the chapter, in the section on leading.

Conflicting commitments

Those who do come on to your project will often have other commitments to manage, as well as your project. You must establish what these are at the outset. Far too often, scheduling takes place on the basis of an assumed 100 per cent availability. Not only does this store up a whole series of awkward negotiations for the future, but it is demoralising for team members to see their other commitments implicitly devalued to zero at the stroke of a pen or cursor. The better approach is to consult at the outset about other commitments and work around these in your planning. That way, people will feel wholly committed to their scheduled availability.

Balancing workloads

Clearly, some team members will be full time and others will offer varying levels of commitment. Workload balancing does not mean giving everyone the same amount of work, but giving everyone an amount of work that they can achieve in the time they have available, without putting them under undue stress. As time pressure increases on your project, it is the stretch and stress you need to balance, to ensure everyone feels they are being treated fairly. There is not much that is as potent in undermining morale on a team as a feeling of unfairness.

What goes wrong?

Projects fail when poor planning does not identify all resource needs, or makes flawed assumptions about skill levels, commitment or availability.

Resourcing tools

The simplest resource planning tool is a *responsibility chart*, which shows three things: what needs to be done, who is available to do it, and the various roles and responsibilities that need to be fulfilled. Two common formats for responsibility charts place slightly different emphasis on the three components.

RACI chart

The first charts roles and responsibilities against tasks. The flexibility of these tools means you can choose the roles and responsibilities that are relevant to your project: maybe electrical work, labouring or supervision. Four of these roles give the chart its popular name in the USA: a *RACI chart*. The figure below shows why. The flexibility also means that, whilst you can allocate people task by task, you can also do so at the level of groups of tasks (or work packages), whole work streams, or even whole projects, where you want a simple overview of multiple projects.

The greenhouse project

RACI CHART

	Responsible	*Authorisation*	*Consult*	*Inform*
Select greenhouse	BK	AJ	Gardening club	Family
Mark out and lay concrete foundation slab	BK	AJ	Bob the builder	Family
...				

Into the RACI chart above, we insert the names of team members who are allocated to fulfil the roles for each task. In the conventional RACI chart:

Responsible   The person who will do the work – or lead it.

Authorisation The person empowered to sign off the work as completed satisfactorily.

Consult   Usually people whose opinion needs to be taken into account in doing the work. Can also mean people with specialist knowledge who can advise on the work.

Inform   People who need to be aware of what is happening and when.

This is your chart now, so adapt it as you see fit. Use different roles, add more, define them differently. Enter as many people into each box as jointly share the role, and choose the level of detail for the tasks, which gives you the visibility you want.

Responsibility grid

The other form of chart, the *responsibility grid*, puts people ahead of roles and starts with the tasks and the people available to you. It is the roles and responsibilities that are allocated into the cells. Each can be written in or represented by a symbol.

RESPONSIBILITY GRID

	Sarah	Harold	Sam	Nick	Meg	Karen	Michael
Task 1	(A)	(S)	(D)			(E)	(D)
Task 2	(A)	(S)		(D)			(D)
...							

Examples of typical responsibilities are:

(A)   Authorisation – or sign-off   (E)   Expert

(S)   Supervision   (C)   Customer

(D)   Doing the work   (P)   Provider (of materials, information, assets …)

I prefer this format to the RACI chart, because it makes it so much easier for team members to see what they are allocated to do. It is also very helpful in workload balancing and can easily accommodate other commitments.

RESPONSIBILITY GRID FOR WORKLOAD BALANCING

	Sarah	Harold	Sam	Nick	Meg	Karen	Michael
Task 1	(A) 2	(S) 4	(D) 8			(E) 3	(D) 6
Task 2	(A) 2	(S) 6		(D) 10			(D) 8
Task 3		(A) 1	(E) 4		(S) 6	(D) 10	(D) 10
Task 4		(A) 2				(S) 6	(D) 12

Other Commit-ments	6	0	12	18	0	12	0
Total	10	13	24	28	6	31	36

In the responsibility grid above, the project manager has worked with each team member to learn their other commitments (in days) and to estimate the work required (in days) to fulfil each responsibility. If this is a six-week, or 30-day, project, then the project manager can immediately see that Karen and Michael are over-committed. Meg and Sarah, however, have plenty of spare capacity. Perhaps Sarah could take over the supervision of task 4 from Karen; and Meg could do the work, along with Nick, on task 2. This would better balance workloads and avoid Karen and Michael failing to deliver.

Organising yourself

You can download a blank responsibility grid, which you can adapt to your own needs, from **www.manageagreatproject.co.uk**

Time-resource chart

A variation on the theme of responsibility charts allows us to schedule work allocations. Neither version of responsibility chart says anything about scheduling, and some project managers either don't like Gantt charts or want to focus on their people. If that's you, the *time-resource chart* is a great tool.

TIME-RESOURCE CHART

	Sarah	*Harold*	*Sam*	*Nick*	*Meg*	*Karen*	*Michael*
Week 1		Task 1	Task 1			Task 1	Task 1
Week 2		Task 1	Task 1			Task 4	Task 1,2
Week 3		Task 2	Task 3	Task 2	Task 3	Task 3	Task 3
Week 4	Task 1	Task 2		Task 2	Task 3	Task 3	Task 3

Sourcing your support

Where will you get your team members from? The first consideration is whether it will be from within your organisation or from an external source – most commonly contracted in, but maybe 'on loan' from a partner organisation, through a secondment or similar arrangement. Interns are another valuable source of project resources and, if you lead them well, projects can offer valuable learning opportunities.

Team members from inside your organisation

Projects draw team members from within their organisation to meet organisational requirements. In doing so, they create a virtual organisation, within the organisation. This sets up tensions of priority and authority. There are different ways that organisations respond, in terms of structuring and delegation to project managers. Let's consider three examples.

Example 1: Business first

Perhaps the simplest structures are where functional or divisional managers appoint project managers who draw all (or the great majority) of their team members from within that manager's domain. This manager has final control, often acting as sponsor, and the project manager has as much authority as the manager grants them. This in turn dictates the relative priority in accessing resources of the project, against business-as-usual activities.

Example 2: Business and projects intermingle

Where projects cross the organisation, drawing resources from all divisions and functions, project managers must negotiate with a range of senior and middle managers for resources. The organisational level and political adroitness of their sponsor becomes a key determinant of their success. The project manager themselves may come from within one of the participating functions or be an outsider – external to the organisation or, increasingly, from a dedicated project management function within the organisation. This latter model implicitly grants the projects a greater measure of authority, but the leadership of that function must carry enough organisational clout to face off against powerful operational function leaders.

Example 3: Project priority

The biggest, most important projects can sometimes assume the scale and organisational status of a function in their own right. When the project leadership is appointed from among the most capable and respected executives, this gives the project significant power in negotiating for resources – although it can easily be seen as a bit of an outsider within its own organisation. Taken to the extreme, some organisations become 'projectised' and are constructed out of many projects as their primary organisational structure.

Contracting team members from outside your organisation

Sometimes you will need to bring resources into your project from outside your organisation. The commonest reasons are the need for specialist skills or not having enough surplus capacity. This offers opportunities and threats.

The primary advantage is your ability to choose specifically the skills you want from a market place, interviewing candidates and being choosy. They can bring with them depth of expertise and breadth of experience. The principal threat is that outsiders do not understand your culture and practices. Whilst this can lend them a certain objectivity, they will need to get things done amongst your colleagues and it will take time for them to build trust. They can often be seen as outsiders, making the project feel alien and therefore threatening to your colleagues.

Having read this far, the secret to effective contracting of project team members (whether individuals or businesses) will come as no surprise:

1 **Know what you want.** Before you speak with potential suppliers, document precisely the skills, volumes and outputs you need.

2 **Establish your case.** It's no good finding a great supplier if internal politics mean that you will be prevented from contracting with them.

3 **Survey the market.** Find a short list of qualified candidates who can all offer excellent qualifications, experience and references. And do take up references properly, in person, speaking to the person, before you sign anything.

4 **Put together a specification and look for a proposal.** Before you issue your brief, determine how you will evaluate proposals. How will you balance different criteria, such as price, experience, innovation, warranties, quality…?

5 **Meet the best.** Nothing beats a face-to-face meeting with people that you will be working with, and on whom your reputation will partly rest. Plan the meeting so you can learn what matters most to you, before making your decision.

6 **Notification.** Notify your preferred candidates first, in case they choose to decline. Once you have their formal confirmation that they are ready to join your team, let the others know, and be prepared to give honest and valuable feedback, if they ask 'Why did you not choose me?'

Projects fail when senior leaders do not give enough organisational commitment to a project, leading to an over-reliance on contractors, consultants and other outsiders.

Managing

As a project manager, you will be up against a deadline, trying to achieve something challenging, with a newly come-together team of people. Yet the biggest challenge is none of these: for most project managers, the people they manage are not in a formal sense answerable to them. You have authority, but no power. This makes day-to-day management seem easy; at least there, you would have all of the levers of reward and punishment at your disposal. As a project manager, often you do not.

So you need to be able to influence actions, without the clout to enforce them. One of the commonest consequences of this is the broken promise: you ask me to do something by the end of the week; I nod and say 'Uh-huh', and we go our separate ways. On Friday afternoon, you ask me 'How did it go?' 'Oh, sorry' I say. 'It didn't get done.' Sound familiar?

The problem is that I never really committed to doing it and you never asked me for that commitment. If Jiminy Cricket is my conscience, then he slept through the whole exchange. If you want a better chance that I will comply, you need to wake Jiminy up. You can do that by alerting me to the fact that you are going to ask me something important: 'Mike, do you have a moment? There's something important I want to ask you.'

Okay, Jiminy has woken up. Now ask me what you want me to do. But here's the key: you need to ask me the question properly. Be confident. When I have said my somewhat evasive 'Uh-huh', look me right in the eyes, so I cannot avoid the situation, and ask: 'So, Mike, will you get it done by 3 pm on Friday?'

You may be worried that I will break the spell and say no. But isn't it better that you know it's a 'no' now, than assume a feeble 'uh-huh' means 'yes', and then get a shock when it's too late? Now you have choices: ask for a later deadline, find out what would stop me and help me manage that commitment, thank me for my time and ask someone else … Lots of choices.

Mike's rules

Treat anything other than an unambiguous 'yes' as a 'no'.

And if I look you in the eye and say 'Yes', then you have a commitment. And now it is backed up by Jiminy Cricket, my conscience. If I find myself getting close to Friday and haven't done it, I am going to start feeling guilty, Jiminy will keep nagging me and, if I possibly can, I'll get it done.

This in no way creates a certainty, but it does raise the odds of my compliance. Of course you may want to give Jiminy a shot of caffeine, to really wake him up. Make the request even more formal; in your office, for example. For an even greater buzz, do it in front of other people, at a team meeting, say. That way, my conscience will be aware that I'd be letting down not just you but my colleagues.

In our culture, the gold standard of commitment is a written signature. When project managers need that certainty, we use a *work package definition* (WPD). This sets out what we expect our colleague to do, and we sign it to say we are assigning that responsibility to them. They sign it to say that they accept that responsibility. Use a WPD when you need an audit trail, have contractual relationships, or simply need to create the greatest levels of certainty. In a less formal environment, an exchange of emails is more common and is perfectly adequate.

Organising yourself

On the page opposite is a sample template for a work package definition. It sets out some of the things you will need to consider. You can download a copy, which you can adapt to your own needs, from **www.manageagreatproject.co.uk**

How to manage a great project

Work package definition template

WP title	Date:

Output required	*List of required deliverables and their key attributes*
Completion criteria	*Required quality controls and approvals*
Activity description	*Functional description of work required, broken down to an appropriate level of detail*
Inputs/dependencies and other resources	*References to known inputs/dependencies, standards and other constraints, available tools and resources*
Estimated effort	*Effort allocated for WBS activities – indicate units used*
Planned timescale	*Date planned for work package completion, and any other milestone dates*

Assigned by:	*signature*	Date:
Accepted by:	*signature*	Date:

Delegation

No project manager with anything other than the smallest project can manage without delegating. The trick is to find the best person to do each job, from the multiple points of view of speed, effectiveness, risk and skills development.

When you have matched the person to the task, brief them well and get their commitment. Then be sure to monitor their progress and give them feedback, encouragement and praise at each achievement.

Tricks of the trade

Management styles

Your people management will be most effective when you match your style to the person's individual needs for the task at hand. Here are four styles and when to choose them.

Telling

For people who are new, lacking experience but enthusiastic, your best strategy is to give clear, straightforward instructions. Only give as much responsibility as they can safely handle, so their first experiences will be successes.

Guiding

For people with a little more knowledge, you may give them a bit more responsibility, knowing that sometimes failure is the best way to learn. But you must guide them well, giving them the instructions that they need, to succeed. And also offer the support that will build their confidence when they struggle with greater complexity.

Supporting

Eventually, people become skilled enough not to need a great deal of instruction. They will need some, but too much guidance will stifle their creativity and growing confidence. But until they become expert at doing what you have set them, they will make mistakes, denting their confidence and reducing their motivation. So your primary strategy must be to be supportive.

Trusting

When you ask someone to do a task they have mastered, any guidance will demoralise them, and too much support will hint at a lack of confidence on your part. Set clear expectations, give them the time and resources they need, and trust them to get on with it. If you are going to stretch someone, if you are going to delegate good quality, demanding work, do so whole-heartedly. When you give people responsibility, you must trust them fully and let them stand or fall on their own performance. By all means put in scheduled reviews where you can recognise and praise progress, and certainly be available for consultation, but the time to get nervous about the risk is before you decide what to delegate, and to whom. Once you have made your decision, trust is essential if you want to maintain enthusiasm.

Leading

There is so much to say about the topic of leadership in projects that I wrote a book about it: *Brilliant Project Leader*. At the core of the book is a simple rule:

Mike's rules

You get the team you deserve.

To deserve the team you want, you need to address the four essentials of team leadership (see diagram overleaf): focusing on individuals, building and sharing a clear plan, fostering a true sense of team spirit and communicating relentlessly – and well.

Focusing on individuals

There may be 'no I in team' but, if there is no sense of individuality, then where is the diversity that gives a team its strength in problem-solving, its robustness in challenges and decision-making, or its joy in learning from one another? Get to know each team member and find out their strengths.

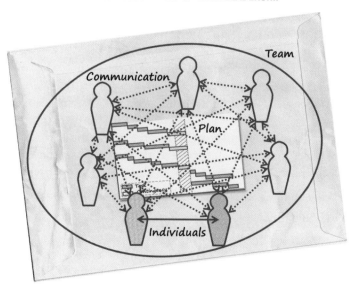

Invest your time and energy in helping each one to develop and grow their skills as a result of involvement in your project. There are two dimensions you can stretch people in: skills and responsibilities. The chance to learn new things and to strengthen existing skills towards mastery is intrinsically motivating as well as good for careers and therefore for employers. And opportunities to take and discharge more responsibility grow character and judgement.

Mike's rules

Value people for what they can offer – rather than deprecating them for what they cannot.

Building and sharing a clear plan

People need the sense of control and certainty that a plan brings. Without it, they can have little confidence in their leader. But it is important to involve your team in creating your plan.

How to manage a great project

It is easy to believe that you have a monopoly on wisdom and foresight when it comes to planning. You don't. There are three compelling reasons to involve team members in planning:

1 Together, you have greater collective wisdom than any one of you alone.

2 Involving people in the planning process is a recognition of their experience, knowledge and judgement – which is highly motivating.

3 When team members get involved in planning, they become more committed to the plan. They have a reputational stake in making the plan work.

Fostering a true sense of team spirit

People need to feel a sense of belonging and a team is ideally placed to provide that. It offers three things we value particularly highly at work: relationships, recognition and respect. So, cultivate a team spirit and the best place to start is where our eight steps start: with a clear goal. A shared and compelling purpose is both motivating and unifying. Add to this a few simple team traditions, like cakes on Friday or celebrating team successes on a Monday morning, and you will bring people together and foster the loyalty, mutual regard and collaborative behaviours that will carry you all through easy times and hard.

Communicating relentlessly – and well

Nothing stifles enthusiasm more than the feeling of not knowing what is going on, what is expected and what the future holds. Create effective communication channels and take responsibility not just for communicating well yourself, but also for building a culture of good, collaborative team communication among team members. Done well, this leads to spontaneous collaboration, seamless conflict resolution and real caring between colleagues.

Motivation

Keep your team motivated by becoming a human environmental control mechanism. Like any environmental controller, use feedback to constantly adjust the levels of support and challenge, and to feed in resources when they are needed. And don't forget to remove unwanted heat and contaminants from your team before they stifle enthusiasm and productivity.

Problems build up and, just like the fizzing bombs in Tom and Jerry, if you don't tackle them quickly, they will explode in your face. Not only does this hurt you and anyone around you, avoiding problems looks weak to your team, and creates a climate of 'What next?' fear. A positive willingness to take on issues rapidly and make decisions will create the confidence in your leadership that motivates followers.

An enthusiastic team will want to work hard for you. What will you give them in return? There is no need for elaborate gifts and bonuses: their role in motivation is exaggerated by the people who have become accustomed to them. Fundamentally, people need to feel valued for their efforts. A three-step process works well:

1 **Recognise their contribution** and help them to learn valuable lessons from their experience.

2 **Reward their efforts** with something as simple as your praise and thanks.

3 **Celebrate their successes** by recognising them in front of their peers.

Here is the most important thing, though. Do not save all your feedback, praise, and opportunities to learn from experience until the end of the work. Build it into the regular cycle of progress checks and support. This way, you can harvest its benefits throughout the life of your team.

Brilliance

People want to follow leaders. So be the leader people want to follow. Define your leadership template to build the style that feels right to you and creates the culture that you want. Integrity is not negotiable, but I would also want enthusiasm and confidence, optimism and flexibility, openness and compassion, challenge and excitement. What will your leadership watchwords be? And how hard are you prepared to work to make them a day-to-day reality; even on the toughest of days?

Lessons from the real world

1 New people can add new ideas, new perspectives and new value. They can also be a pain in the neck to integrate into your team. Introduce them when you need more resources or you need to disrupt your team's thinking.

2 When you know what capabilities you need, your main job is to find the very best people you can find, who have those capabilities.

3 The chicken and the pig decided to convert the farmer from bacon and eggs to muesli. Hire more pigs for your team.

4 Choose people with strong opinions and create opportunities to hear them debate with other people with different opinions. Well-managed creative differences can avert disasters.

5 It is far better to be one person down in your team than it is to knowingly take the wrong person in a desperate bid to maintain numbers.

6 Make sure that people look you in the eye and commit the time they have offered you.

7 Your first meeting with your new team members is your best chance to create a positive relationship. Prepare well and learn people's names.

8 Save micro-management for exceptional cases only. Scale your management style to meet each person's needs and to address the level of risk.

What if it goes wrong?

Step 6

Essential practices of Step 6

1 Identify and analyse threats to your project.

2 Develop plans to mitigate threats and deal with contingencies.

3 Implement your plans with vigour.

Things go wrong

Things go wrong: let's take that as a given. No matter how good your plans are, they will not be a complete representation of reality, which is prone to uncertainty.

Risks are uncertain events that can impact upon your outcomes. In particular, we focus on those events whose effects are adverse: the threats. So Step 6 is all about identifying and managing those threats. We shall follow a simple four-part process for doing this.

RISK MANAGEMENT PROCESS

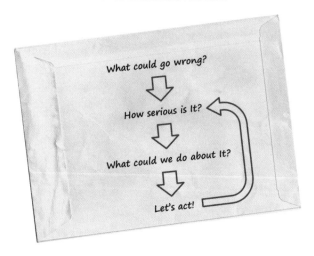

What could go wrong?

⬇

How serious is It?

⬇

What could we do about It?

⬇

Let's act!

Mike's rules

Shift happens!

This is Mike's first rule of life. Things change, the unexpected happens and, if you are not ready for shift, then you will not be in control of your project.

How to manage a great project

Prevention is better than cure

Before you start with our four-part process, you should be thinking during your planning process of how you can prevent risks from occurring. A good framework is to consider threats to:

→ **Your schedule.** Your primary defences against schedule problems are scrupulous checking of the logic you apply to sequence and dependencies, robust evaluation of your estimates, and applying suitable contingency periods to absorb slippage.

→ **Your budget.** Your cost breakdown structure (CBS) is the best tool for making sure you have missed nothing and for reviewing budget estimates. Add budget contingency at an appropriate level of your CBS.

→ **The quality of what you will deliver.** Plan quality into your project with quality design, quality assurance and quality control processes. Consider a quality specification that exceeds requirements by a small margin, to allow for occasional errors.

→ **Your ability to deliver the full scope of your project.** Your work breakdown structure (WBS) is your main method of getting scope right. Plan your delivery schedule to deliver the most important elements of scope first, to lock them in early on and reduce the risk of under-performance. Set up a rigorous process to manage requests for changes once scope and specifications are agreed. You will learn about this at Step 7.

What could go wrong?

Mike's rules

Project failures are often a result of the TYFTA: the Thing You Forgot To Ask.

The first part of our *risk management* process is fundamentally about asking the question 'What could go wrong?' Wouldn't it be great if your most sceptical colleague were with you now, to tell you all the things they can foresee? If they are, great. If not, you need to get a group of people together to brainstorm all the risks. Capture all the ideas, so that you can then move on to the next part of the process and evaluate how serious each one is.

Tricks of the trade
Pre-mortem

One way to help find things that could go wrong is Gary Klein's *pre-mortem* method. Here, we ask people to imagine the project is over … and it has gone horribly wrong. Ask them to write down what has happened. This overcomes what is known as the *planning fallacy*: our tendency to believe our plans and hence to find it hard to spot flaws in them. Instead, what you have done is told people the plans were flawed and allowed their innermost concerns to emerge.

Once you have a list of potential failures, take them one at a time and get the group to list all the things that could have caused it. Repeat for each failure mode and you have a good list of threats to your project.

Another way to identify things that can go wrong is to look back on past experiences, previous projects and, if available, schedules of typical risks. Specialist books like my own *Risk Happens! Managing Risk and Avoiding Failure in Business Projects* have long lists of the sort of things that can go wrong on projects. Take one of these and add to it as a valuable resource that you can return to time after time.

Useful checklist
Typical generic sources of risk

✔ Complexity
✔ Novelty
✔ Unrealistic expectations
✔ Integrating project assets or processes with existing ones
✔ Security

- ✔ Inappropriate or missing performance measures
- ✔ Poor governance processes, leading to weak oversight and decision making
- ✔ Communication failures
- ✔ Stakeholder resistance
- ✔ Lack of commitment from key people
- ✔ Illness or absences
- ✔ Health and safety
- ✔ Weather or natural disasters
- ✔ Equipment failures
- ✔ Industrial action (lawful or otherwise)
- ✔ Political or legislative changes
- ✔ Changes to market place or competitive forces
- ✔ Supply failures
- ✔ Commercial disputes
- ✔ Funding shortfalls
- ✔ Price shifts
- ✔ Negligence or criminal acts

What goes wrong?

Projects fail when people focus entirely on what they know and fail to consider what they don't. This leads to over-confidence in plans and processes.

How serious is it?

The second part of our risk management process is to evaluate each of the risks you have identified. The two most important questions to ask about each potential risk are:

1 How bad would it be, if it happened?
2 How likely is it to happen?

How bad would it be, if it happened?

This is the easier of the two questions. What you need is a consistent scale that makes sense to you and your team, in the context of your project. Simple adjectives rarely work well, because people interpret words differently. An example would be:

1 OK

2 Awkward

3 Bad

4 Terrible

5 Disastrous

The simplest effective approach is to start with the effect of the risk on the project outcome. An example scale might now be:

1 We'd fix things and cope with the problems.

2 We'd need to shift priorities and change things as we go.

3 We'd need to rethink how we could deliver.

4 We'd deliver, but miss one or more of our objectives.

5 We'd fail to deliver the project.

However, you may be interested in one aspect of the consequences, or another. Here are examples of the impact on budget, schedule and your reputation. Your job is to define your own scales.

Budget

1 We could deal with it without using any contingency.

2 We'd use some of our contingency.

3 We'd use a lot of our contingency.

4 We'd use all of our contingency.

5 We'd blow all of our budget and contingency and need to find more.

Schedule

1 There will be no or very minimal delays.

2 Delays will be within our contingency.

3 We would be overdue, requiring rescheduling of a range of other activities.

4 We would be significantly overdue, adversely impacting on other important initiatives.

5 We would be hugely late, affecting the value of what we deliver or our organisation's reputation.

Reputation

1 Nobody will take an interest in this.

2 Local or trade commentators will note our problems.

3 This will be a big deal for local or trade press – they will lead with it.

4 National press and media will pick up on this.

5 National press and media will lead with this story.

How likely is it to happen?

Estimating *likelihoods* of uncertain events is almost impossible, so the best thing you can do with this aspect of risk is keep it very simple. Few project managers have sufficient understanding of probability and statistics, nor a database of evidence with which to estimate likelihoods robustly. A simple three-point scale would look like this:

1 **Low likelihood:** little or no need to worry.

2 **Medium likelihood:** we need to plan for this.

3 **High likelihood:** seems to happen a lot, so let's prioritise it.

If you must use a more sophisticated approach, here are three tips:

→ Avoid descriptive terms like rare, seldom, possible, probable or likely. At least five research studies show that interpretations of these terms are so wide as to render them useless.

→ Avoid percentage estimates, unless you have both a good data set as evidence and good understanding of statistics and probability theory.

→ Use no more categories than you use for estimates of impact.

Combining likelihood and impact

A useful graphical representation combines the impact and likelihood of project threats on to a chart like this:

RISK ANALYSIS CHART

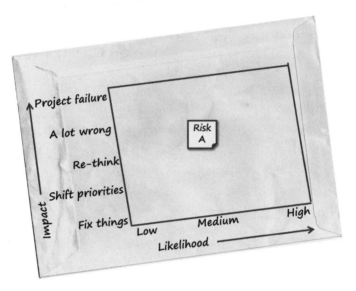

On this chart, the further towards the top right hand corner we plot a particular risk, the more serious it is. We can allocate each risk a single measure of its seriousness by giving the impact and likelihood levels a numerical score and then multiplying the two numbers together. Simple 1, 2, 3, 4 … scoring is the most common approach, although I prefer to recognise that, if each level is considerably worse than the last, a 1, 2, 4, 8 … approach gives a better representation of the real seriousness. But do note that this approach is not mathematically rigorous. You should use it only as a guide to your prioritisation.

Another approach is simply to define colour-coded regions of the chart, like red, amber and green. Both approaches are illustrated in the chart opposite.

RISK ANALYSIS SCORES

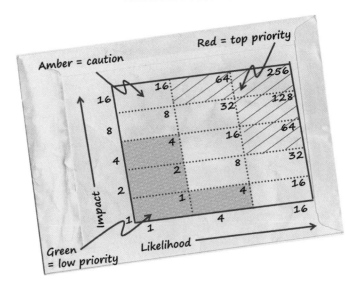

On this chart, you might interpret the three regions like this:

Green   Minimal threat. No plan needed. Respond appropriately if
threat materialises.

Amber   Significant threat. Create and implement a robust plan to
manage the threat.

Red   Serious threat. Create a plan with multiple strands, and
consider cancelling the project if no suitable mitigations
are available.

A chart like this, drawn on a flip-chart or whiteboard, creates a simple
way to engage team members in the risk process. Write each threat
on to a sticky note and use the collective judgement of your team to
allocate it to a spot on the chart. Once you have done this exercise,
you can then start at top right and work with your team, or allocate
responsibilities, to devise plans for what to do about each threat.

What could we do about it?

The third part of our risk management process is to devise a plan for dealing with each risk. There are six strategies from which you can build your plans. I will use examples from that very high-risk activity – driving: 'What can you do to manage the risk of a motor vehicle accident if you are driving?'

The six strategies

Strategy 1   **Eliminate the risk.** This is the best approach, if you can find a way to implement it. Often the only way to do so is to not undertake the risky activity. Therefore, you are most likely to use this for risks you have classed as top priority, red, if other approaches fail.

Examples: don't go out, leave your car at home and take public transport.

Strategy 2   **Mitigate the effects.** Look for ways to reduce the impact, should the risk occur.

Examples: wear your seat belt, drive carefully, reduce your speed.

Strategy 3   **Take preventative measures.** These do not eliminate the risk, but they do make it less likely to materialise.

Examples: drive slowly, drive when the roads are less busy, avoid distractions like mobile phones, drive when you are fully alert.

Strategy 4   **Share the risk.** If you can get someone else to take the some or all of the consequences, your risk is reduced. To make this legally enforceable, you need a contract, and this is the basis of all professional services.

Examples: pay for delivery, take out driver's insurance.

| Strategy 5 | **Have a Plan B.** Whilst this won't make the risk any less serious, it will give you the confidence to know what to do should the risk happen, and that you will be able to contain consequent damages. It is formally known as a *contingency plan*. |

Examples: invest in recovery services, emergency kits, first aid training.

| Strategy 6 | **Do nothing.** For a serious threat, this is an arrogant, foolish, and dangerous strategy. But many threats are minor in terms of both impact and likelihood, and the costs of the other strategies are disproportional to the threat. So a considered decision to accept the risk and tackle it if it occurs is a reasonable strategy. An implicit decision that comes about because you fail to evaluate the risk properly is negligent. |

Example: driving knowing that, despite wearing a seatbelt, being careful, and having insurance and contingency plans, you could have an accident every time you get in a car.

The greenhouse project

Risk analysis – late delivery of building materials

Impact: terrible	Delay could delay concrete laying into period when frost could occur every night
Likelihood: low	Materials needed are standard cement, sand and paving slabs, which are continuously in stock
Total threat level	Amber
Actions	Identify back-up alternative builders' merchant

Organising yourself

On the page overleaf is a sample template for a risk action plan. You can download a copy, which you can adapt to your own needs, from **www.manageagreatproject.co.uk**

Risk action plan template

Risk title		Risk ID no.	
Risk originator		Risk owner	

Section 1: The risk

Risk description			
Evaluation	Likelihood	Impact	Score

Section 2: Risk response

Action plan	
Timing/schedule	
Budget	
Resources (assets and materials)	

Section 3: Residual risk

Contingency arrangements	

Risk register

Your main tool for managing risks is a *risk register* – a log of all the risks that you identify and what you are doing about each. Your risk register serves two principal purposes:

1 It provides an audit trail, demonstrating what risks you have identified, how you have assessed them, what your response plan was and, crucially, what you actually did about them.

2 It is a management tool that allows you to consider what risks you need to focus on, who you need to speak with and what you need them to do.

Organising yourself

On the page overleaf is a sample template for a risk register. You can download a copy, which you can adapt to your own needs, from **www.manageagreatproject.co.uk**

Many project managers are quick to develop and populate their risk registers. But once they have their risks and risk plans entered, they seem to forget about them. If you do nothing, nothing will change. You need to actively work on your risk register, ensuring that tasks are done, risks are re-evaluated and, where necessary, further action is taken.

Let's act!

Keep risks at the forefront of everyone's mind. Include discussions of new risks emerging and what is being done to manage existing risks at all project meetings and reviews, so you can constantly reduce the overall risk to your project.

Ensure that the people allocated responsibility for each risk are working through their plans and assessing the need for further action. Speak with them frequently and update the entries to their risks on your project risk register.

Risk register template

Risk ID	Author	Date identified	Description – include cause and consequences	Likelihood score	Impact score	Total risk score	Countermeasures	Risk owner	Planned close-out date	Progress	Actual close-out date

Impact scores	Very high: 16	High: 8	Medium: 4	Low: 2	Very low: 1
Likelihood scores	High: 4		Medium: 2	Low: 1	

Calculate **total score** by multiplying **likelihood** × **impact**

If at first you don't succeed ... try something else.

Sometimes your corrective actions will not reduce the risk to an acceptable level where 'do nothing' remains as your only required strategy. So be sure to come up with a new plan and put that into action. It is this constant cycling back that is the secret to success.

A risk becomes an issue

A risk becomes an issue when it becomes a certain event: either it will happen or it has happened. You must deal with issues as quickly as you can – but not more quickly than is prudent. Step back and evaluate the situation, to understand as clearly as possible what the issue is, what its consequences may be and how important it is. Then examine all your options, looking for the one that is most effective, but at a cost that is proportional to the impact of your issue. Once you have made a decision, act quickly and precisely, keeping alert to the effects of what you are doing, so that you can stop if they are not what you need, and reconsider your approach.

Closing out risks

As your project progresses, you should be able to close out risks. There are four ways this can happen:

1 The most satisfying is when, thanks to effective management actions, the risk is no longer a threat.

2 The passing of time may also have rendered the risk harmless.

3 You may delete the risk from your register, because you recognise that it is poorly defined, and you replace it with one or more better-defined risks.

4 The worst case is when the risk has materialised and you have had to deal with the consequences.

Lessons from the real world

1 Always have a crisis plan for what to do if the biggest project disaster occurs.

2 Always expect the unexpected. I don't think it's original advice (it is not – Monty Python, Oscar Wilde and Heraclitus got there first), but it remains good advice.

3 Most risks can be spotted if you ask the right question. The secret is to ask a lot of questions … and not to stop asking until the project is complete.

How is it going?

Step 7

Essential practices of Step 7

1 Monitor performance against schedule.

2 Monitor performance against budget.

3 Analyse variances and implement remedial action plans.

4 Record and report on status.

5 Control the pressures to make changes.

6 Prepare for and provide training to integrate the solutions, products or processes into business-as-usual operations.

7 Rehearse for the key period when change will occur – often called handover or go-live.

8 Conduct regular meetings to identify lessons that can be incorporated into daily practices.

Sitting on a sofa

Do you recall the four stages of our project roadmap?

Stage 1	Define your project
Stage 2	Plan your project
Stage 3	Deliver your project
Stage 4	Close your project

Having completed Steps 1 to 6, you have done everything you need to do to define and plan your project. You are ready to deliver it.

You have done the difficult bit: now it's time to get a cup of coffee, find a comfy chair, kick back and relax. The Delivery stage is where you hand over to your team of helpers and leave them to it. In fact, on one project, my boss came up to me one day and said, 'Mike, what exactly do you do on this project? Whenever I pass by, you seem to be sitting on that sofa, drinking coffee, chatting to one of your team leaders.'

'Well,' I said, 'I spend most of my time sitting on this sofa, drinking coffee, chatting to one of my team leaders.' My team leaders and I had spent a long time defining what the project was about and planning it carefully. We'd thought about what could go wrong, whom we needed to keep informed and how we were going to allocate work. Now it was their job to lead the people doing that work, and it was my job to keep those teams co-ordinated, to support my team leaders, and to have a clear idea how it was all going.

And the best way to do that was to chat with those team leaders a couple of times a day – on the sofa, with a coffee – and wander around speaking to team members and reviewing the work they were doing.

Know which hat you are wearing

I know that most of you will not have the luxury of being a full-time project manager. And still fewer will work with large enough teams to have full-time work stream leaders, leading teams of full-time staff. But here's the thing: when you are a project manager who also has responsibility for delivering parts of your project, this means that you have to wear two different hats: your project manager's hat, and your team member's hat.

Mike's rules

When you need to wear two hats, wear only one at a time.

So you will almost certainly have two hats to wear during your project. You may even have more, if you are working on other, non-project, activities. The most important thing is to wear only one at a time and to know which one it is. If you are wearing your project manager's hat, focus on the management side of the project. When you are wearing your delivery hat, get on with that job. Multi-tasking is not efficient and it is not effective. It leads to stupid mistakes and errors of omission.

Watch, understand, intervene

As project manager, your first role during the Delivery stage is to be aware of everything that is happening, so that you can understand how your plan is playing out and how reality is diverging from your expectations. Your next job is to find ways to intervene to bring your project back on plan: to catch up with your schedule, to keep within budget and to deliver what has been promised. When all is going well, these interventions need only be subtle tweaks of timing and allocation of work. In tougher times, you will be solving challenging problems and making difficult decisions.

This process is called the *monitor and control cycle* and is illustrated below.

THE MONITOR AND CONTROL CYCLE

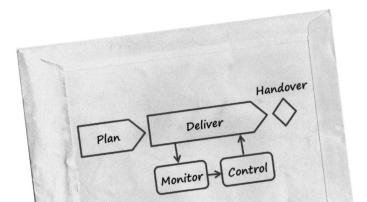

The single most important thing to know about the monitor and control cycle is 'rhythm'. If you go around the loop fast enough, then you will catch problems and discrepancies early, while they are still small. You will be able to fix them with subtle interventions and you will be able to assess the effectiveness of your choices quickly and tweak them if they are not working. You will stay in control. (Remember the rule from earlier: 'The one thing a project manager craves, above all else, is control'.)

If, on the other hand, you cycle around the loop too slowly, you will only spot problems when they have grown large. You will need to make big, risky interventions to get your project back on track, but you will only find out how successful you have been after a significant delay. Your project can easily spiral out of control.

How to manage a great project

Mike's rules

An absentee project manager is a contradiction in terms.

Let's start with the two parts of the monitor and control cycle, before looking at your other main areas of concern during the Delivery stage: reporting, controlling change, leading the project and delivering what you promised.

Monitoring

Watch and understand your project's progress both formally and informally. Formally, you need to:

→ Compare progress against your schedule. If you have them, you will use your milestones and Gantt chart.

→ Compare expenditure against your budget.

→ Assess your deployment of people and how they are performing.

→ Evaluate the draw-down of material resources and utilisation of assets.

→ Monitor for new threats to your project and assess the effectiveness of risk management actions.

→ Assess the quality of deliverables that are being produced.

Informally, you also need to:

→ Stay aware of what stakeholders are saying about your project and infer their attitudes to the things that are happening.

→ Gauge the mood of your team, by speaking with people and listening to their triumphs, their setbacks and their concerns.

Mike's rules

Your level of attention to detail can make the difference between success and failure.

Whilst a lot of your formal monitoring will be based on empirical evidence, it is also highly dependent on communicating effectively with your team. Your informal monitoring will be entirely dependent upon that.

Project team communication

In my time as a project manager, I have experienced four different models of project team communications. Let's examine them one at a time.

Me-me

Don't you just hate people who hoard information to themselves, treating it as a precious asset which they alone are qualified to manage? It is not only annoying, though: it is dangerous. We all work at our best when we have good quality information to base our decisions on, so the 'me-me' communicator can never be a truly effective project manager.

Me-you

The 'me-you' communicator makes it their business to ensure everyone else has full access to any information that is not specifically privileged by confidentiality or sensitivity. Working with this kind of project manager gives you a feeling of confidence and trust and, whilst it is a burden to hear bad news about your project, it is far better to hear it openly and accurately than to suspect it, hear rumours of it, yet to never know for sure.

Mike's rules

Knowledge is not power, but it is empowering.

You-me

On a well-run project, the project manager will rarely be the first to know everything that goes on. Your team members are hard at work with clients, with colleagues; developing ideas, products and processes. They are encountering challenges and making

How to manage a great project

breakthroughs. It is they who get much of the information first. So the 'you-me' communicator prioritises listening to their colleagues to gather and synthesise a fuller understanding, which they can then disseminate in a 'me-you' manner.

You-you

The only problem with 'you-me' communication is that you can become the single point of failure. Whilst an absentee project manager is a contradiction in terms, you will sometimes need to step away, leaving someone else to monitor and control your project. But what will happen to team communication if you are not there to act as its focal point? The 'you-you' communicator recognises this problem and establishes a culture of open communication where everyone makes it their business to disseminate the information they have and collate the information they need.

Project meetings

Do you run or attend team meetings? I bet you do, from time to time. What happens when the team leader is not there? If the meeting goes ahead without them and functions just as efficiently, this is a true 'team meeting'. If, on the other hand, it gets cancelled, curtailed or functions poorly, then what you really have is a 'team leader meeting'.

Establish regular formal team meetings – which will take place whether you can attend or not. Create a structure for them, which includes issuing an agenda, allowing sufficient time to complete it, expecting people to arrive on time (and starting on time even if people are missing) and respecting participants enough to finish on time.

Set the tone by arriving early, being well-prepared and keeping comments concise and relevant. Document your meetings and quickly issue a list of actions people have committed to and decisions that were taken.

Projects need these formal team meetings – but not that often. Far more often, you need to gather people together for a quick update, to work on a problem, to prioritise among emerging issues, or to allocate responsibilities. These kinds of meetings should be whenever you need them, never without a specific objective, and as brief as they can be, while still accomplishing their aim.

Have meetings standing up. Better yet, have them in informal spaces like around a coffee machine, in a lift lobby – anywhere convenient but not so comfortable that people settle in and savour them. Their job is to get something discussed and agreed, and the quicker you can do it the better. Some projects also benefit from a regular daily, or less frequent 'morning stand-up' that updates people on progress since the last one and prioritises work for the next period. They can be strong team-development events, but keep them short and snappy.

On one project I worked on, half a dozen senior managers, each leading a big work stream, would get together at 8 am around the coffee machine to share and discuss concerns. It went on regardless of who had other commitments and kept that small team tight and well co-ordinated. It took no more than 10 to 15 minutes, which we would no doubt have spent getting a coffee anyway.

Controlling

Your mission is to keep your project under control and so deliver your promised products on time and within budget. As you find problems, variances or other issues, you must address them as soon as you can. Some of us have a tendency to recoil from these sort of issues and hope that they will go away on their own: they rarely will.

Mike's rules
Fizzing bombs have a tendency to go off in your face if you don't put them out.

The monitor and control cycle will usually keep you on track, as long as you go around the loop frequently enough to stay in control. But sometimes events can take over. You may have missed this event in your planning through negligence, haste, poor assumptions or maybe just because it was truly unforeseeable. The fact is that sometimes no amount of cycling between monitor and control will get you out of your hole. And when in a hole: stop digging.

How to manage a great project

Re-planning

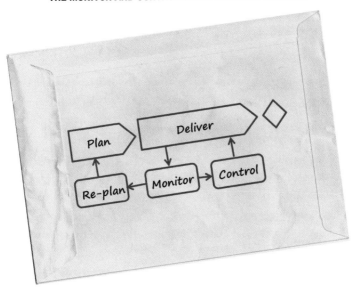

When the monitor and control cycle no longer allows you to feel in control, the best thing to do is to stop. Stop work on any aspect of your project about which you do not have 100 per cent confidence that it is doing the right thing. Re-focus your resources on three questions:

1 **Where precisely are we?** Without a definitive understanding of your situation, you cannot proceed with any confidence.

2 **Where are we now aiming to get to?** This may or may not have changed since the start of your project.

3 **What is now the best way to get there?** Build a new plan against which you can monitor and control progress.

Sometimes we build a period of re-planning into our original plan. Where there is a point of significant uncertainty in your project, you can easily feel like you will lose control. So schedule a period of re-planning following the point where that uncertainty is resolved. This is the time when you will regain control of your project and be able to move forward to the next phase with certainty.

Project controls

You learned at the start of Step 4 that your plans describe how you will deliver your project, and your *controls* will show how you will work to your plans or, if you cannot, how you will manage the process of reverting to them or building new ones.

Useful checklist

Twelve common project controls

- ✔ **Stage boundaries.** This is the principle control mechanism to ensure good governance of your project, which we covered in 'How managing a great project works'.

- ✔ **Checkpoint meetings.** You may want to constitute review meetings at key stages in your project, to examine progress, performance, delivery, risk or other priorities.

- ✔ **Risk and issue management.** We looked at these in detail in Step 6.

- ✔ **Schedule control.** This is managed within the monitor and control cycle, primarily by re-allocating resources and re-scheduling tasks.

- ✔ **Budget management and cost control.** This is also managed within the monitor and control cycle, primarily by making judgements about the relative priorities of budget, schedule, scope and quality.

- ✔ **Document management.** How you reference, store, maintain and make available the documents your project produces or relies upon.

- ✔ **Version control.** How you ensure that the status and currency of documents, processes, software, specifications, etc. are unambiguous and easily found. Document version control is easy to manage, yet often neglected. A version of the manuscript of this book might be labelled: *'How to Manage a Great Project v0-11 d26-02-13 eMC'.* The version is 0-11 – the 11th draft (0 means draft) dated 26 February 2013 and edited by MC – Mike Clayton. The first approved copy would be v1-00 and, as soon as it is amended, would become v1-01.

- ✔ **Configuration management (CM).** CM goes beyond version control and applies to technology – both hardware and software. It records not only versions but what the versions can and cannot do, do and do not contain, and how they are and are not compatible with other components of a wider system. The intention is that changes which are found not to work fully can be readily unwound, allowing a system to be returned to a stable configuration.

✔ **Project reporting.** We will examine this in the next section, 'Reporting'.

✔ **Change control.** We will examine this in the section, 'Controlling change'.

✔ **Quality reviews.** We will examine this in the section, 'Delivering what you promised'.

✔ **Handover.** Handover marks the end of the Delivery stage and the start of the Closure stage. We will cover this in 'Step 8: How did it go?'

Reporting

Project managers don't tend to be the sort of people who enjoy sitting down and writing reports. So why bother?

→ Because you have a duty to notify certain people of the status of your project.

→ Because you may need to maintain an audit trail of events, decisions and outcomes.

→ Because team members work best when they have a comprehensive understanding of the state of your project.

→ Because stakeholders will pay attention to rumours, speculation and gossip in the absence of good information.

These reasons are all important. They are about good governance and good communication. But for the busy project manager there is one reason that feels a lot more compelling: it will help you to do your job better. Put more objectively:

→ Because there are people who have access to resources you cannot command, who have wisdom that exceeds your own, and who have the authority to make decisions that you cannot make. And you need to access all of these, to help you control your project.

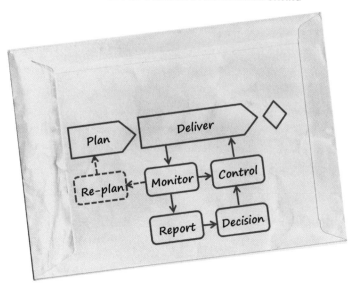

There are two types of report that you will use during the Delivery stage: progress reports and exception reports.

Progress reports

A *progress report* is the standard way of updating on a range of project-related topics – typically progress against schedule and budget, risk profiles, use of resources and delivery of products, along with forecasts and issues. At the start of your project, work with your most important stakeholders to understand what information they will want and how they will want you to present it, so that you can design a standard report template that you can use during delivery. Also decide upon a reporting cycle: will it be weekly, fortnightly or monthly? On what days or dates will it be issued? From this, you can build a reporting process that allows you and your team to gather, collate and analyse the data, interpret it and prepare a report that presents it clearly, along with a narrative that sets out the essential messages your sponsor, client, board and important stakeholders need to understand.

Tricks of the trade
RAG status

Project managers often present a summary of each area of their project in the form of *RAG* or *traffic light* status. RAG stands for Red, Amber, Green.

Green status   Everything is going according to the plan – or close enough to be within an agreed tolerance, such as 5 per cent of outstanding budget or remaining schedule.

Amber status   There are known problems, but they are both within a wider agreed tolerance (such as 15 per cent) and, crucially, you have a plan to remedy those problems.

Red status   The project is not at green status and you do not have a plan to recover that status or, whether you have a plan or not, the variance is too great for an amber status.

Organising yourself

On the page overleaf is a sample template for a progress report. You can download copies of this and other formats, which you can adapt to your own needs, from **www.manageagreatproject.co.uk**

Exception reports

Exception reports do not come at a predictable time; they reflect unexpected adverse events and need to set out plainly what has happened, what it means, the options for handling it and your recommendation. Because there is often an urgency attached to the issue, writing your report should not be your first move. First, speak directly with the people you need to consult: your boss, sponsor, director or client. Use the report to formalise and document that discussion and its outcome.

Progress report template

RAG status:	**RED / AMBER / GREEN**

Headlines

Tasks, milestones, outcomes scheduled for this period		Completion dates	
Tasks, milestones, outcomes	Comments	Plan	Actual / forecast

Major risks and issues

Budget status

Recommendations and requests for decisions or support

Tasks, milestones, outcomes scheduled for next period		Completion dates	
Tasks, milestones, outcomes	Comments	Plan	Forecast

Author	Date

Organising yourself

On the page overleaf is a sample template for an exception report. You can download a copy, which you can adapt to your own needs, from **www.manageagreatproject.co.uk**

Controlling change

Everything is going well, and then someone has to spoil it: 'Mike, you're doing well. Great. The only thing is ... I've changed my mind.' This is the prelude to a request for you to change some aspect of the project: the scope or specification of what you are delivering.

As a project manager, you are probably a can-do sort of person who instinctively says 'yes' to any challenge like this. The problem with this is that your original scope and specification have been approved by a thorough process: where is the robust examination of this request – or the authority to accede to it? Perhaps it is better to say 'no'. But this itself is problematic: the person who is asking may have spotted a genuine need. External conditions change, mistakes are noticed, better solutions become available: what if they are right?

Remember: what you crave is control, so the answer is a robust *change control process*.

On receiving a *change request*, thank the requester and ask them to document two things that they are best positioned to do:

1 The precise details of the change they would like.

2 The reasons or benefits for the change.

Once you have this, you and your team can set up the other side of the business case for the change. You have the benefits, now evaluate the costs: the incremental cost, resources needed, impact on schedule, change in risk profile and effect on other activities. Only with this information can you expect a decision maker to make a reasoned decision.

Exception report template

What has happened?	Describe the circumstances that triggered the need for an exception report.
What are the implications?	Describe the expected or possible outcomes if no action is taken. Include the impacts on budget and on schedule.
What are the options?	Describe the options for resolution, along with their costs and resourcing implications.
What are the effects of the options?	Describe how each option will affect the outcome, along with implications for the time, cost and quality of the planned project outcomes.
Recommendation	Describe the project manager's recommended solution (along with any warnings not described above).

Author		Date	

For subsequent completion

What action was taken?	
What was the outcome?	
Who authorised this?	It is possible that the project manager has authority to resolve the issue on their own.

If their decision is 'yes' then the proposer is happy and you have all the resources and time you need. If it is 'no', then at least the proposer can understand that the decision was made in a transparent and accountable way.

THE MONITOR AND CONTROL CYCLE WITH CHANGE CONTROL

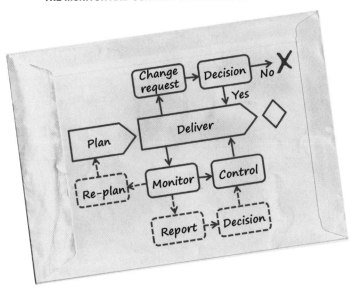

Organising yourself

On the page overleaf is a sample template for a change request. You can download a copy, which you can adapt to your own needs, from **www.manageagreatproject.co.uk**

It is a good idea to keep a *change log*, tracking all the change requests you receive, the decisions and their implementation status. This will give you an audit trail of how and why your finished project differs from that originally approved.

Organising yourself

On page 175 is a sample template for a change log. You can download a copy, which you can adapt to your own needs, from **www.manageagreatproject.co.uk**

Change request template

Enter short title for proposed change here	CR no.*	

Proposer: Enter name here	Date

Description of proposed change	
Reasons for change/ benefits	

Reviewer: Enter name here	Date

Budget/cost impact	
Schedule/time impact	
Resource requirement	
Impact on other projects/activities	
Risks	

Sign here to authorise

Authorised by: Enter name here	Date

Approved ☐	Deferred ☐	Rejected ☐

Reasons	

* Change request number allocated by the change controller

Change log template

CR no.	Change description	Proposer	Submission date	Reviewer	Review date	Authoriser	Approval date	Approval status*	Implementation status

* Approval status: ✓ Approved ✗ Rejected ? Deferred

Leading the project

In this section, I want to consider your role throughout the Delivery stage of your project, where time and pressure can make extraordinary demands. Let's think about the exciting, the mundane and the exceptional.

The exciting: create a buzz

In *Brilliant Project Leader*, I discuss the importance of creating the kind of buzz around your project that draws people to it and energises your team. I call it a 'brilliant project' and offer tips at each stage. It is the job of every project manager to be a leader and to create a brilliant project.

Useful checklist

Twelve ways to create a buzz around your project

- ✔ Let people know why your project matters: what it will achieve and the difference that will make.
- ✔ Articulate a compelling shared goal for your project and your team.
- ✔ Promote your project wherever you can, speaking passionately about it to anyone who will listen and writing about it wherever appropriate.
- ✔ Use pilots and prototypes to demonstrate what you can achieve, to counter your critics, and to motivate and excite your supporters.
- ✔ Build a team that cares, collaborates and communicates well, by investing your time and energy in supporting and encouraging each one of them.
- ✔ Look for opportunities to innovate and create new ideas.
- ✔ Never accept 'OK' when excellence and spectacular are options. The standards you set yourself will rub off on your team.
- ✔ Always put on your 'leadership face' when you walk through the door. Confident, smiling and optimistic outlooks inspire and motivate because your team will take their emotional lead from you.
- ✔ Be there for your team, ready to collaborate with them and support them. Be generous with everything that matters most: your praise, your trust and your time.

✔ Have the courage to do what you believe is right for your project *and* for your team. Never make the mistake of thinking that these two priorities will conflict: when you have the right team and you lead them well, the two needs come into complete alignment.

✔ Your absolute integrity is never negotiable. Trust others if you want them to trust you and always act as if your next choice will determine everybody's trust in you.

✔ Take every reasonable opportunity to recognise and celebrate achievements.

The mundane: keeping on top of things

In the busy rush of managing a project, it is easy to lose sight of the mundane tasks that are absolutely necessary. And under the pressure of events, even project deadlines can slip your mind. So you need to be organised and disciplined in your personal time management.

Useful checklist

Seven things you must pay attention to

✔ Forthcoming project milestones.

✔ Your own personal list of things to do.

✔ Fizzing bombs.

✔ What is around the next corner – are there things you have not yet noticed?

✔ The quality of your team's work.

✔ Maintaining your relationships with team members and stakeholders.

✔ Your personal admin and the all-important project admin.

The exceptional: getting back on track

Crises are often the result of over-confidence: in planning, procedures, people, and your ability to spot dangers. Before you know it, your project can be way off track and you need to handle it. Remember, trade-offs between schedule, budget and quality will not answer your problems, but they will help you to define them.

Under pressure, many of the 'rules' of project management need to become subservient to pragmatism. You need to find your own balance between rigour and realism.

Useful checklist

Ten pragmatic ways to accelerate your project

This is not in any way intended to be a prescription. Consider each option on its own merits in the context of your own situation and 'handle with care'.

- ✔ Set aggressive deadlines.
- ✔ Work extended hours (and ask others to, too).
- ✔ Reduce the rigour of task and product definitions.
- ✔ Trust people to do things right, with less need for pre-approval.
- ✔ Put other, non-project priorities to one side.
- ✔ Trade budget for additional resources.
- ✔ Reduce the scope of your ambition.
- ✔ Buy in packaged solutions.
- ✔ Increase your tolerance for certain types of risk.
- ✔ Reduce planning to a framework and rely on experience and judgement.

Delivering what you promised

When you reach the end of the Delivery stage of your project, there is a very simple question you will need to address: 'Are the things you have produced fit for purpose?' If you can demonstrate that the answer is 'yes', then you will be able to hand them over to your client, customer or whoever will take day-to-day responsibility for them, and move to Step 8 and close your project down.

If you cannot show that your work is fit for purpose, the best you can hope for is a negotiated extension to your time and maybe your budget, to put things right. Perhaps you will end up in a nasty dispute, trading recriminations and maybe even resorting to the courts: yuk.

Of course, if you did your job right at Step1 and you accurately defined and documented what was required, then what you produce will be judged against that. If you did not, then you will almost certainly be found wanting, because there is no objective way for you to prove you have done your job properly. Investing time in defining and specifying project outputs and outcomes is never wasted.

Quality control

The last stage of your quality processes is *quality control* (QC) – evaluating what you have done against its specifications and standards. It is not an ideal process, because anything that is found wanting needs to be re-done in some way, incurring additional cost. It is far better to get your quality assurance right and for everything to pass QC. The benefit of QC is that, if something is wrong, it will be you who finds out about it and it is therefore you who will have control of your choices. Quality control may not be ideal, but it is better than failure.

Lessons from the real world

1 Don't over-commit your time with too many tasks: leave time to manage.

2 If you work for a big organisation – especially one in the public sector – maintain an audit trail of every significant event and decision. A project diary is a great way to record this.

3 A pretty coloured RAG report means nothing to a black-and-white printer, or a colour-blind client. Always spell out status.

4 Set tolerance triggers for exception reports in advance. This way, you need not waste time wondering 'should I or shouldn't I?'

5 Scope will creep and specifications will change, so have a process to manage this ready from the outset.

6 Testing and quality control should be a part of your strategy, not a last minute add-on. Plan testing at each part of your development cycle.

7 What are you doing to ensure the quality of every deliverable? These are what you will ultimately be judged by.

How did it go?

Step 8

Essential practices of Step 8

1 Secure handover, and document any post-handover requirements.

2 Conduct a final evaluation of lessons that can be learned from your project.

3 Review the outcomes of your project and the performance of your project team.

4 Complete all outstanding project administration tasks.

5 Recognise, acknowledge, publicise and celebrate your project's successes.

Handover

The Delivery stage of your project ends, at least in principle, with the handover of your deliverables to the new owner. 'In principle' because, in practice, you should have been handing over deliverables throughout the Delivery stage, rather than storing them all up (and therefore storing up all the risk) until the last moment.

So, in practice, the *handover* at the end usually marks handover and signing off of the last deliverable. On technology projects, this may also mark the switching on, or 'go-live' of the new system. Once again though, this is more principle than practice. In reality, project managers would want a period of stable operation before seeking formal sign-off.

Whenever handover occurs, it not only marks the end of the Delivery stage, it also marks the start of the Closure stage. Whilst you may think that everything is done, there are specific things to do, to close the project formally and consider it done.

> **Mike's rules**
>
> If it isn't right, it isn't finished.

So, in Step 8, we will look at three things you need to do to close your project down in an orderly fashion:

1 Review your project.

2 Complete your admin.

3 Celebrate your success.

We can't seem to finish

Before we look at the three things you need to do to close your project, let's start by acknowledging that this can be a challenging time for a project manager.

Being 99 per cent complete can be pretty demotivating for people who typically like action and change. If there is so little action left and all the change is accomplished then project managers and their teams easily get bored and hanker after other, more exciting challenges. Sometimes they will take the opportunities that arise, leaving colleagues in a depleted team towards the end of the project. As project manager, you need to manage this. Of course, as project manager, you are not immune from this and it may be you who are seduced to your next project, leaving your last one unfinished and lacking direction in its final days.

These problems weaken project team resolve and can also extend to the governance tier of the project. This can open you up to unpleasant lapses in administration, like sudden pushes for additional changes at the last minute, buyers trying to get more from the project than they have commissioned, or even regretting their commission and looking for excuses to reject some aspects of your work. If the original commissioner goes, the new one may even look for excuses to reject and renegotiate your original brief. Project team members may, themselves, seek to re-write history to cover up project failings, asserting later implementation schedules than were originally planned, or justifying poorer results, for example.

And then there is the general ennui that can make the end of a project feel like a dripping tap that you can never quite turn off. Nobody can really be bothered to do the last things necessary to bring it to a close. So you need simple and effective strategies to handle these challenges.

Strategy 1 **Manage team exits.** Actively help team members find a suitable next project. That way, you will know what is going on and be better placed to agree transition and timing. Look for ways to replace key team members who leave early, including board members. On a successful project, a chance to join that success, even for a few weeks, can be appealing to people. One particular thing to look out for is people who relish the detail of finishing off things 'just right'. In the Belbin® Team Roles model, these are people whose team role preferences include 'completer-finisher'.

Strategy 2 **Manage your own exit.** If you need to leave before the project is completed and closed, then make sure you appoint and brief your successor. You can make arrangements to run the closing of your project from a distance, popping in from time to time, but my experience is that this is rarely a happy way to end your project for you or for your team. Your divided loyalties will inevitably be drawn towards your new team and your old team will sense your waning enthusiasm. You will effectively leave on a low note, cancelling out a lot of the high notes you worked so hard to create. A clean break is usually best.

Strategy 3 **Manage change requests.** You have a process for managing requests for change. Operate it rigorously until the very end.

Strategy 4 **Manage formal handover.** This becomes more important if clients have changed or if their mood has shifted. Formal handover can only ever be really well managed when you have a formal specification that was signed off at the end of the Planning stage. If I didn't get across the importance of this at Step 1, let me reiterate: without an agreed detailed specification, you have no firm basis to demonstrate that your deliverables are fit for purpose and therefore that the new owner, operator or user has no choice but to accept responsibility for them

Strategy 5   **Publish performance measures.** Re-writing history is not just a problem in repressive regimes; it happens at the end of all but the most successful projects. You may be tempted to do it yourself, but always consider the long term. These things have an inevitability to them: it will get out and once your reputation for integrity is damaged, you will never truly recover it. So publish all performance measures at the outset, track all approvals for changes to them, and publish final performance measures after delivery. What clients and employers really want in a project manager is not a 100 per cent success record (although that would be nice), but an ability to understand why projects perform as they do and to apply that understanding to improve the performance of your next project.

Strategy 6   **Award medals.** Use small rewards like campaign medals to recognise and incentivise attendance and contribution on your project. Consider creating a 'to the bitter end' medal for the last team members left standing, on the very last day. Make this a real badge of honour.

Strategy 7   **Turn the end into a project.** If tidying up loose ends is less exciting than a project, create a 'finishing project' to close off those last details. Assign it to someone who will see it as a worthwhile challenge: a junior team member eager to show that they can plan and deliver a series of important tasks. If you clearly state what needs to be done, it is easier to get on with it.

Strategy 8   **Create a hard end date.** Commit to a hard end date, and then publicise it, so there is nowhere for you and your team to hide. Then celebrate it.

Learning lessons

At the end of your project, there are four things you need to review:

1 **How did your project go?** This is sometimes referred to as a project *post mortem*.

2 **What did we learn from doing it?** This is sometimes referred to as a project *lessons learned*.

3 **How did each team member perform?** You need to give your team members individual feedback on their performance.

4 **How did the outcomes compare to the benefits you projected?** This happens after your project is closed.

Project review

There are three questions that tend to be addressed at the end of a project: 'Who?', 'What?' and 'Why?' The question of who grabs the glory and who gets the blame is often uppermost in people's minds, but it is by far the least important – and you know it. The truth is that you as project manager must give the glory to your team and put your hand up for any blame: that is the burden of leadership.

But understanding what happened and why are far more important so that you and your organisation can learn and adapt. One of the most important areas to inquire into, for the benefit of the organisation, is estimates: of time, budget and resource utilisation. Organisations and project managers frequently get this wrong, and then make the same mistakes again!

If your purpose is primarily to reflect on how well the project went, then a conventional set of questions is likely to suffice:

→ **What did we intend to achieve?** Start with your scope, quality, schedule and budget specifications.

→ **What did we actually achieve?** Make an honest appraisal of what really happened.

→ **What were the causes of what happened?** Because the questions 'How?' and 'Why?' are of more use than simply 'What?'

→ **What should we do the same and what different, next time?** This moves you towards ...

Lessons learned

The value of a lessons learned review is not in the neat document you produce at the end, but in the quality of the stories, folklore and rules of thumb that your project generates. These are what individuals take with them through their careers, while your carefully produced report sits on a high shelf gathering dust, only to be re-filed in the round filing cabinet on the floor, when people move office or job.

If you want to focus on lessons that you can learn, you will want a more reflective process than your project review. Three good questions to ask are:

→ 'What ideas, contributions or events made the most difference to the project?'
→ 'What were the most surprising events and outcomes?'
→ 'What would be your priorities on day one of a similar project?'

What your people most need is to consolidate the skills they have used, and turn them into positive reputational assets. The biggest mistake people make in any kind of review is to only focus on what went wrong. If you are familiar with the framework of *appreciative inquiry* this is a good way to conduct your review.

In a nutshell, appreciative inquiry is a process of asking questions that uncover positive potential by finding and celebrating the best of what is, and imagining what might be.

Useful checklist
Twelve ways to promote a learning culture

✔ Make learning an on-going part of your project at project meetings, starting at Step Zero.
✔ Keep an on-going record of lessons you and your team are learning, throughout the project – both what works, and what does not. This *lessons learned log* will not only improve practices, but will give people credit and kudos for contributing to it.
✔ Focus on learning, not blaming.

▶

✔ Celebrate positive learning.

✔ Use the lessons learned process to help people develop, and prepare for the next steps in their careers.

✔ Encourage people to keep a *continuing professional development* (CPD) record while participating in your project. Make it clear that informal learning is of equal value to formal learning like training and reading.

✔ Be prepared to accept criticism of your own behaviour, decisions or actions.

✔ Focus on what matters most: don't let nit-picking details dominate your agenda.

✔ Ask: 'What is specific; what is generalisable?'

✔ A great exercise is to ask people to write: 'Advice to my younger self'.

✔ One-to-one chats can be a valuable way to open up personal lessons.

✔ Involve other stakeholders (like suppliers, partners, colleagues, customers) in your learning process.

Even if the value of a lessons learned review does not lie in a formal document, many organisations will want one, and creating one can also focus minds. If just one person reads it, a *lessons learned report* can still make a difference to a future project. Weigh up the pros and cons of investing the time and effort but, if you do decide to prepare one:

→ Be sure to focus on positive lessons.

→ Include an assessment of how significant each suggestion is.

→ For each suggestion, also consider the contexts in which it is valid.

→ Ensure that team members receive full credit for the innovations and insights that contribute to your report.

Organising yourself

On the page opposite is a sample template for a lessons learned log. You can download a copy, which you can adapt to your own needs, from **www.manageagreatproject.co.uk**, along with a template for a lessons learned report.

How to manage a great project

Project lessons learned template

Unique ID	Date	Author	Lesson learned	Recommended actions	Person responsible for action

Individual feedback

As a project manager, you are not just the manager of your project, but of your people too. And your last formal responsibility to each of them is to offer recognition for their achievements, thanks for their contributions, praise for their efforts and good quality feedback on how they can take their experiences and use them as a sound base for the next step in their careers.

Outcomes review

You cannot conduct a meaningful review of the outcomes of your project immediately after completion, because it will take time for the impacts to be felt and the benefits to accrue. So your responsibility at this stage is to schedule a review of the outcomes at a suitable time after handover or go-live. Typically, this will be after anything from six to eighteen months. Choose the longer end of the range only if you really do need the time to establish a sufficient base of information to evaluate, because the sooner you do your review, the sooner you can take remedial actions if they are needed.

At that review, ask: 'How do the benefits achieved by your project match up to the benefits you planned in your business case and project definition?' If your project has not achieved its planned benefits, you will need to assess what corrective actions you need to commission in order to achieve more of the planned benefits.

Organising yourself

On the page opposite is a sample template for a project completion report. You can download a copy, which you can adapt to your own needs, from **www.manageagreatproject.co.uk**

Mike's rules

Nobody likes admin; if they did, they'd call it fun.

How to manage a great project

Project completion report template

Success in delivering outcomes/deliverables	
Impact of approved changes	

Baseline completion date:	Actual completion date:	*Comments and reasons for any variance*
Baseline budget cost:	Actual cost:	*Comments and reasons for any variance*
Baseline quality specifications:	Final quality specifications:	*Comments and reasons for any variance*
Baseline planned benefits:	Actual benefits delivered:	*Comments and reasons for any variance*

Lessons learned from the project	*The purpose of this section is to advise other projects about your experiences, good and bad. For example:* • *Were initial estimates accurate? If not, why not?* • *Were the testing activities effective?* • *What tools were most successful?* • *What would you do differently next time?*
Recommendations for future projects	

Author	Date

Closing down

Projects seem to spawn admin and, whilst nobody likes doing it; it is necessary. So make a list and get on with it. Use people who like getting things completed or who feel that taking the admin on can help demonstrate their capabilities, and ensure that you don't arrange your celebration until after the admin is done.

Useful checklist

Common project closure admin tasks

Project management

- ✔ Formally close out all risks and issues.
- ✔ Produce and sign off operational use memo.
- ✔ Conduct project review.
- ✔ Produce and sign off formal project closure memo.

Financial and contractual

- ✔ Set a deadline for submission of final expenses and timesheets and check them in.
- ✔ Pay outstanding invoices.
- ✔ Complete a summary of all costs against budget.
- ✔ Close down any project cost codes that are no longer needed.
- ✔ Check that all requested and approved contract changes have been documented and agreed to.

Staff

- ✔ Release team members to other roles.
- ✔ Ensure that all team members update appraisals and career plans.
- ✔ Conduct performance reviews formally if required – otherwise, ensure you give informal feedback.

Communications

- ✔ Make internal and external announcements that the project is complete.

Contractors, consultants and temps

✔ Debrief to identify what knowledge they have of lasting value to you. Ensure that all knowledge is documented.

✔ Agree leaving dates with each contractor and notify consultancies or agencies.

✔ Review the individual's performance for the agency and to act as a basis for any future reference.

✔ Ensure final invoices are met.

✔ If a temp or contractor is transferring to another department, ensure charge will be made to the appropriate cost code.

✔ Check that all contractors, consultants and temps hand back keys and security passes.

Information and data

✔ Archive information for future use. File and index all project files, working papers and data.

✔ Ensure network and email data is backed up and accessible.

✔ Determine who has responsibility for archives.

✔ Ensure that all confidential waste is properly dealt with.

Operational use memo

An *operational use memo* serves as the handover guide to any process, procedure or asset. At its simplest, it may be an instruction manual, but it may also contain commissioning guidance, maintenance routines and role descriptions. It must provide anything that the new owner needs to know. Often it also includes the sort of checks and procedures that are needed to ensure snags are noted and dealt with while the new process or asset becomes familiar.

Organising yourself

On the page overleaf is a sample template for an operational use memo. You can download a copy, which you can adapt to your own needs, from **www.manageagreatproject.co.uk**

Operational use memo template

Recommendations for follow-on actions and notes of unfinished work or potential problems, for the manager responsible for a product or asset in operation.

Product or asset concerned	

Outstanding risks	*Outstanding risks to be monitored that may affect operational use or lifetime*
Changes to specification	*Changes to the original specification*
Actions to be completed	*Actions (such as approved changes) that have not been completed*
Any other recommendations	

Author:	Date
Accepted by:	Date

Sign here to accept

Saying thank you

Mike's rules

Always, always, always celebrate your successes.

When your team celebrates, they will feel good about their achievements, taking that confidence with them into their next role. That confidence will boost their performance, which will get better results. With better results, they will be able to celebrate more: celebration creates a virtuous cycle of improvement.

Make the scale and the nature of your celebration consistent with the project, the culture of your organisation, and the personalities of your team. It can be anything from cakes with Friday afternoon tea, to a meal out, to an expensive team event away from site. As long as it is equally accessible to all, and fits with the prevailing culture, it can work.

Useful checklist

Ten ways to celebrate project success

✔ Personal thanks to team members from you, the project manager, and from senior colleagues.

✔ A visit to the project from a celebrity (national, local or organisational).

✔ Posters placed prominently, celebrating your success.

✔ Articles in magazines and on websites.

✔ A drink, a meal, a party.

✔ Gifts, tokens or souvenirs – the financial world uses resin-embedded notices known as *tombstones* to mark important transactions.

✔ A conference or formal event.

✔ Entry of your project into a competition that showcases best practices or great performance.

✔ Talking about your project in meetings, conferences and interviews.

✔ An awards ceremony for your team.

And yes, you could also offer …

✔ Bonuses and promotions for your team members.

Project closure memo template

This project has been completed:

☐	Testing has been completed satisfactorily	Date
☐	Acceptance criteria have all been met	Date
☐	All project administration is completed	Date
☐	Project review is completed	Date
☐	Lessons learned review is completed	Date
☐	Operational use memo is completed and accepted	Date
☐	Project outcomes review is scheduled for …	Date

Comments

Prepared by: *Enter name here*	Date

Signed:

Authorisation

I am satisfied that this project has been completed.

Authorised by:	Date

Signed:

Project closure memo

When you have celebrated your success, there is only one thing to do. Complete a formal *project closure memo* that states you have handed over successfully, done your reviews and completed your admin and now consider your project closed. If your boss, your client, or your sponsor countersigns that memo, you're finished.

Organising yourself

On the page opposite is a sample template for a project closure memo. You can download a copy, which you can adapt to your own needs, from **www.manageagreatproject.co.uk**

Lessons from the real world

1   Schedule project review meetings in advance, put them in diaries, and make them mandatory.

2   A snagging list is not enough to prevent handover – as long as the requirements fall within normal operational practices.

Learn the lingo

As we have been through the eight steps that guarantee you will be in control of your project, we have introduced a lot of project terminology and jargon. Knowing this jargon will not make you a better project manager, but it does provide a quicker way to communicate with other project managers who know it. So, here is a summary of all of the essential project lingo hat you will need, to get by.

We will start, inevitably, with **project**. A project is a co-ordinated set of tasks that together create a defined new product, process or service, within a constrained time and resource budget. A **project manager** is that circus performer who can keep juggling relationships with the many people involved in the project, whilst keeping many tasks spinning like plates. A good project manager must be able to get things done, organise people and processes and succeed at influencing, motivating and inspiring their teams.

Projects are divided into **stages**, or phases, to help us manage them and, in this book, we worked with four basic stages: Definition, Planning, Delivery and Closure. Between these are **stage boundaries**, also known as stage gates, gates or gateways. These are review points where we make go or no-go decisions based on how the project is performing and the value we will get from our further investment.

The purpose of the Definition stage is to define what the project is and is not. To do this we must establish a **goal** or aim for the project and a set of **objectives**. These set out how you will measure your success in achieving your goal and are typically expressed in terms of time, cost and quality, forming the **time–cost–quality triangle**, also known as the triangle of balance, triple constraint or, in the USA, the iron triangle. To protect our ability to deliver to schedule, budget and standards, we often include some **contingency** in each so that, if the unexpected occurs, we have some room for manoeuvre.

The 'fourth corner' of the time–cost–quality triangle is **scope**. This sets out how much work we need to do and how much our project will produce. An inevitable pressure, which project managers work hard to counter, is for people to add work to our project; a process known as **scope creep**.

The things our project produces are called **deliverables** or **products**. They are sometimes also called outputs and are the physical or intellectual things the project produces. They can be contrasted with **outcomes**, which are the real-world changes

– beneficial, we hope – that result from the **integration** of our deliverables into how we do things. That task is sometimes the role of a distinct **integration manager**.

We aim to define our deliverables as precisely as we can, with detailed **specifications**. These derive from a good understanding of the **requirements**; both quality- and functionally-driven. To help us prioritise these, we use **MoSCoW** analysis, setting out the musts, shoulds, coulds and won'ts from among people's quality and functional requests.

Quality is so important to projects that we have three essential processes to draw from: **quality design** is getting the right quality into the specifications and design of the deliverables; **quality assurance** is the way we carry out delivery to make sure we produce them to the designed standards; and **quality control** is the process of checking that deliverables meet the required standards before we release them to our client.

All this goes into a **project definition document** also known as a project charter, project terms of reference (TOR), outline project initiation document (PID), or project brief. The acronym **DCARI** reminds us to also include the dependencies between our project and other activities, the external constraints upon our project, the assumptions we have had to make and will need to test, the risks or threats to our project, and any issues that we need to resolve.

We need to demonstrate that, if we do our project, it will offer good value for money and that the benefits will outweigh the costs. The tool for this is an **investment appraisal**, which examines the two and shows as objectively as possible how they compare. This often gets wrapped into a larger document that is a piece of advocacy for the project and is called a **business case**. It is good practice for a business case to compare a number of different project options, to give decision makers a real choice. One option should be the **do nothing option**. Another important consideration is **benefits realisation** – how you will make sure that the project will achieve the benefits promised in the business case.

Projects need to be accountable, and this is managed through **governance** processes. The two chief roles of governance are: oversight to ensure the project is performing as it should, and decision making. The most prominent person in this role is the **project sponsor** who acts as a decision maker, overseer, counsellor to the project manager and conspicuous advocate for the project. They are supported by a **project board** or **steering group** that consists of the right mix of people to help with evaluating the project and making decisions. Steering groups are sometimes advisory, and feed their comments into the board.

Perhaps the most important people to a project manager are the **stakeholders**; those people, groups or organisations who have an interest in the project. A good project manager will actively manage their stakeholders, identifying who they are, understanding them, planning a series of messages and how to deliver them, and then following up assiduously.

At the outset of planning a project, we start to build one comprehensive document that encompasses all our planning. This is called the **Book of the Plan**, the project initiation document (PID), the project terms of reference (TOR), a master plan or, sometimes, a project bible.

There are many planning tools, but perhaps the simplest is the **milestone**, a fixed point in the project schedule when something has happened – usually the completion of a task or the creation of a deliverable. **Type 1 milestones** are the big points in the project we use to start planning and they mark significant points along the way. **Type 2 milestones** are smaller achievements that we use to track progress and so give us an indicator of how well we are keeping to schedule.

A whole family of valuable tools starts with a systematic documentation of all the work that needs to be done in a **work breakdown structure (WBS)**. From this, we can allocate people to tasks, to create an **organisational breakdown structure (OBS)** and we can put cost estimates against each activity to build up a project budget in the form of a **cost breakdown structure (CBS)**. The deliverables can be documented in hierarchical format in a similar way, to create a **product breakdown structure (PBS)**.

If we take the activities from our WBS and arrange them into a logical sequence, we create a **network chart** that allows us to plan out the sequence of tasks. Specific methodologies distinguish a generic network chart from its two cousins, which both include durations of the activities: a **PERT chart** (PERT stands for program evaluation and review technique) and a **critical path analysis**. The

critical path is the longest route through a network chart and is critical in the sense that a delay to any of the activities on this path will delay completion of the project.

A related chart is the more widely used **Gantt chart**. This places the focus on duration and time, rather than on logic and sequence. It represents each activity by a bar whose length represents the duration of the activity and whose placing shows when it is scheduled to start. When one activity must follow another, this is known as a **dependency**, and if there needs to be a gap between one activity finishing and the next starting, the gap is called a **lag**. If an activity can finish late without affecting the rest of the scheduling, this is called **float** or sometimes, more colloquially, **slack**.

Powerful tools for planning what people we need and how we will use them are **responsibility charts**, and two common forms are the **RACI chart** – where RACI stands for four common roles of responsible, authority, consultation and informed – and the **responsibility grid**, which is more formally known as the **linear responsibility chart (LRC)**. We can allocate specific chunks of work in a formal manner, using a document called a **work package definition (WPD)**.

Risk management is a vital aspect of project management that recognises the importance of anticipating and dealing proactively with the things that could go wrong. A **risk** is an uncertain event that could affect outcomes. The level of uncertainty is measured by the **likelihood** or probability of the risk, and the effect on outcomes is measured by its **impact** or sometimes severity. The latter term, however, only implies the scale of the impact, whilst the term 'impact' captures both the severity and nature of the effect. We tend to focus on **threats** – risks with a negative impact.

The process of risk management has four steps: **identify** what could go wrong, **analyse** how serious it is, **plan** what we can do about it and take **action**. Where we cannot sufficiently reduce a serious threat, we need to plan what we would do if it came about; this is a **contingency plan**. Risks are recorded, along with our analysis, plans and a record of our actions, on a **risk register** or risk log.

The beating heart of the Delivery stage is the **monitor and control cycle**. We observe what is happening on our project, compare it with our plans, and make interventions and corrections to bring everything back on schedule or budget. To help us stick to our plan or get back to it, we use **project controls**. There is a list on page 166, but the most important are often risk management, **reporting** and **change control**. The two types of report we produce in the delivery stage are: **progress reports** (also known as highlight reports, summary reports or project updates) and **exception reports**. Progress reports set out a broad spread of essential information on project status and tend to be prepared on a regular cycle at predictable times. Status is often summarised with a **traffic light report**, or **RAG status**; allocating red, amber or green status to project activities depending upon their performance – from good performance according to plan (green) to poor performance that deviates substantially (red). Exception reports are issued when something exceptional happens, and they document the incident and how it is to be handled.

Change control is the process of managing **requests for change** to make sure decisions are made accountably. The requests are documented on a **change request** form, and all requests are logged and tracked on a **change log**.

The Delivery stage ends with the final **handover** of the last of the deliverables to their new owner. This also marks the start of the Closure stage. Handover of the deliverables is often accompanied by an **operational use memo** that sets out the information the owner needs to know. The project team can then carry out a number of reviews, finish off any outstanding admin tasks and then celebrate the completion of the project. Final completion can be marked and formalised with a **project closure memo**. Then all that's left is to switch off the lights and go **home**.

Good fortune!

Mike's rules

Fortune favours the prepared mind and the carefully planned project.

Very often, good fortune is of our own making. But it takes hard work and careful consultation to set up the conditions for success. No one can guarantee you that – even if you do everything right. But that is not the offer of *How to Manage a Great Project*: what I offered was that, if you follow my eight steps, you remain in control of your project. You can never be in control of events but, by doing the right things and by doing them well, you will increase your chances of success. This is what the best project managers do, day after day, all over the world.

Mike's rules

Simple is not easy.

Most of the tasks in *How to Manage a Great Project* are simple: they don't require great learning or vast experience. But simple is not the same as easy, and the best project managers know that they have to work hard, constantly, to hold back the chaos of events and maintain control. But if there is one rule that will best assure your success if you follow it, it is this:

Mike's rules

Do the basics. Do them well and do them relentlessly. And follow through on commitments.

If you do the basics, you do them well and you do them relentlessly, you will set up the conditions for success. You will stay in control of your project and you will, I hope, experience good fortune.

All the very best

Mike.

How to manage a great project

Glossary

Assumption – Something you believe to be true, without evidence. There is no harm in making assumptions (it is often necessary). What you must do, is to make your assumptions explicit and test any upon which significant outcomes depend.

Benefits realisation – How you will make sure that the *project* will achieve the benefits promised in the *business case*.

Book of the Plan – At the outset of planning a *project*, we start to build one comprehensive document that encompasses all our planning. This is called the Book of the Plan, the *project initiation document (PID)*, the *project terms of reference (TOR)*, a master plan or sometimes a project bible.

Budget – We need to demonstrate that, if we do our *project*, it will offer good value for money and that the benefits will outweigh the costs. The tool for this is an *investment appraisal*, which compares the two and shows as objectively as possible how they compare. This often gets wrapped into a larger document that is a piece of advocacy for the project and is called a *business case*. It is good practice for a business case to compare a number of different project options, to give decision makers a real choice. One option should be the 'do nothing option'.

Business case – An analysis of the benefits and costs of making a change to the way things are done. See also *budget*.

Change control – The process of managing *requests for change* to make sure decisions are made accountably. The requests are documented on a *change request* form, and all requests are logged and tracked on a *change log*. It ensures that where changes are authorised, appropriate additional resources are allocated.

Change log – Document for recording all *requests for change*, their approval status and progress.

Change request – See *request for change*.

Closure – The last stage of a *project*, where the project *team* carries out a number of reviews, finishes off any outstanding admin tasks, and then celebrates the completion of the project. Final completion can be marked and formalised with a *project closure memo*.

Constraints – Limitations on what you can do.

Contingency – An amount of time, budget or functionality incorporated in the plan beyond the *project* team's best estimate of what is needed, to allow for the adverse impact of *risks*.

Contingency plan – A plan developed to mitigate the outcome of a *risk*, once the risk has materialised.

Controls – How you propose to stick to your *plan* in the face of the challenges of the real world, and what you will do when reality forces your *project* to deviate from plan.

Cost breakdown structure (CBS) – Hierarchical presentation of *project* costs, usually derived from the *work breakdown structure (WBS)*.

Crashing the timelines – Making compromises to advance work ahead of schedule, or to catch up a significant delay.

Critical path – The longest route through your *network chart*, representing the duration of your *project*. It is 'critical' in the sense that these are the activities that carry the risk of delay – if any of these activities were delayed, your whole project would miss its deadline.

DCARI – An acronym to remind us to also include the *dependencies* between our *project* and other activities, the external *constraints* upon our project, the *assumptions* we have had to make and will need to test, the *risks* or threats to our project, and any *issues* that we need to resolve.

Definition – The purpose of the Definition stage is to define what the *project* is and is not. To do this we must establish a *goal* or aim for the project, a set of *objectives* and the *scope*. All this goes into a *project definition document*.

Deliverable – The things our *project* produces are called deliverables or *products*. They are sometimes also called outputs and are the physical or intellectual things the project produces. They can be contrasted with *outcomes*, which are the real-world changes – beneficial, we hope – that result from the *integration* of our deliverables into how we do things.

Dependency – Some tasks can get done at any time and are independent of other activities. Others are linked to events like the start or completion of other tasks. These linkages are called dependencies.

Exception report – A report that is issued when something exceptional happens. It documents the incident and how it is to be handled.

Float – The amount of time an activity can be delayed by, before it impacts upon the completion of another activity or, indeed, the whole *project*. It is also known as *slack*.

Gantt chart – A tool, popularised by Henry Gantt, that helps a *project manager* to plan, communicate and manage a *project*. It shows project activities as horizontal bars, with a length that represents the duration of the task, and places them against a fixed time line.

Gate or **Gateway** – See *stage boundary*.

Goal – States the over-arching purpose of the *project* – what you seek to achieve. Also known as 'aim'.

Governance – *Projects* need to be accountable and this is managed through governance processes. The two chief roles of governance are: oversight to ensure the project is performing as it should, and decision making.

Handover – The Delivery stage ends with the final handover of the last of the *deliverables* to their new owner. This also marks the start of the Closure stage. Handover of the deliverables is often accompanied by an *operational use memo*, which sets out the information the owner needs to know.

Home – A place that professional *project managers* visit from time to time. It provides respite from work and a place to get their laundry done.

Impact – The change of *outcome* resulting from a *threat* or opportunity.

Integration – The process of combining the *products* of your *project* with the day-to-day activities or assets that the products have to work with. This task is sometimes the role of an *integration manager*.

Integration manager – The person responsible for making the *products* of your *project* work with everything those products need to work with.

Investment appraisal – Compares the benefits with the costs of your *project*, and shows as objectively as possible how they compare.

Issue – A problem the *project* faces: an issue is technically a *risk* with 100 per cent *likelihood* – that is, one that is certain to occur.

Likelihood – A measure of the probability of a *risk* occurring – often based on an interpretation of how often similar risks have occurred in comparable past circumstances. Therefore sometimes referred to as 'frequency'.

Linear responsibility chart (LRC) – Chart showing responsibilities for each *team* member, against a list of tasks or *work streams*.

Milestone – There are many planning tools but perhaps the simplest is the milestone: a fixed point in the *project* schedule when something has happened – usually the completion of a task or the creation of a *deliverable*. Type 1 milestones are the big points in the project we use to start planning and they mark significant points along the way. Type 2 milestones are smaller achievements that we use to track progress and so give us an indicator of how well we are keeping to schedule.

Mitigation – Any action designed to reduce the *likelihood* or *impact* of a *risk*.

Monitor and control cycle – The beating heart of the Delivery stage is the monitor and control cycle. We observe what is happening on our *project*, compare it with our *plans*, and make interventions and corrections to bring everything back on schedule or *budget*. To help us stick to our plan or get back to it, we use project *controls*.

MoSCoW – An analysis of users' *requirements* from among people's quality and functional requests, in terms of the Musts, Shoulds, Coulds and Won'ts.

Network chart – If we take the activities from our *work breakdown structure (WBS)* and arrange them into a logical sequence, we create a network chart that allows us to plan out the logical sequence of tasks. Specific methodologies distinguish a generic network chart from its two cousins, which both include durations of the activities: a *PERT* *chart* (PERT stands for program evaluation and review technique) and a *critical path* analysis. The critical path is the longest route through a network chart and is critical in the sense that a delay to any of the activities on this path will delay completion of the *project*.

Objective – How you will measure your success in achieving your *goal*. Objectives are typically expressed in terms of time, cost and quality, forming the *time–cost–quality (TCQ) triangle*. To protect our ability to deliver to schedule, *budget* and standards, we often include some *contingency* in each, so that if the unexpected occurs, we have some room for manoeuvre.

Operational use memo – Sets out the information the owner needs to know. It is prepared to support *handover*.

Organisational breakdown structure (OBS) – Hierarchical presentation of project *team* members, according to the work they are allocated to. Derived from the *work breakdown structure (WBS)*.

Outcome – The real-world changes – beneficial, we hope – that result from the *integration* of our *deliverables* into how we do things.

PERT chart – A specific form of *network chart*; PERT stands for program evaluation and review technique.

Plans – How you intend to deliver your *project*. Plans address the three project elements – tasks, time and resources – and describe what needs to be done, how it will be done, when, by whom, with what assets and materials, and how it will be paid for.

PRINCE2™ – PRojects IN Controlled Environments. The UK government's methodology for *project management*. It is maintained by the Cabinet Office.

Product – Also called *deliverable* or output, the things that the *project* produces (physical things or events).

Product breakdown structure (PBS) – Sets out all the *products* (or *deliverables*) of your *project* in a structured way – hence articulates the *scope* of your project.

Programme – A portfolio of *projects* and initiatives managed together – sharing something critical like joint *objectives* or a common resource pool.

Programme evaluation and review technique (PERT) – An estimating technique that starts with a *network chart* and combines optimistic, best estimate and pessimistic estimates to produce an overall estimate of the most likely duration and standard deviation (spread of likely durations) for a *project* activity.

Progress report – Sets out a broad spread of essential information on *project* status. Progress reports tend to be prepared on a regular cycle at predictable times. Status is often summarised with a *traffic-light report*, or *RAG status*.

Project – A co-ordinated set of tasks, which together create a defined new *product*, process or service, within a constrained time and resource *budget*.

Project board – Governing body of a *project* – ultimately responsible for the oversight and decision making. Sometimes called the 'project steering group'; *steering groups* can sometimes have another role.

Project brief – See *project definition document*.

Project charter – See *project definition document*.

Project closure memo – Final completion can be marked and formalised with a project closure memo.

Project definition document – Also known as a 'project charter', 'project terms of reference', outline *project initiation document* or 'project brief', a project definition document contains the definition of your *project*, and therefore sets out the definition of what the anticipated project is (and is not).

Project initiation document (PID) – Formal name within *PRINCE2*^{TM} of the full suite of *plans*, *controls*, *budget*, *specifications* and *business case*.

Project lifecycle – Sequence of *stages* of the *project* from beginning to end.

Project management – The process of managing a *project*. Deploys tools, processes and attitudes that deal with the complexity and uncertainty inherent in a project.

Project manager – A circus performer who can keep juggling relationships with the many people involved in the *project*, whilst keeping many tasks spinning like plates. A good project manager must be able to get things done, organise people and processes and succeed at influencing, motivating and inspiring their *teams*.

Project sponsor – Also referred to as the 'project executive', *SRO* or 'project director'. The project sponsor represents the needs of the organisation to the *project* and the needs of the project to the organisation. They act as 'manager' to the *project manager*. Part of the project *governance* process, the sponsor will either contribute to, or be wholly responsible for, oversight and decision making. They are supported by a *project board* or *steering group*.

Project terms of reference (TOR) – See *project definition document*.

Quality – Quality is so important to *projects* that we have three essential processes to draw from: *quality design*, *quality assurance* and *quality control*.

Quality assurance – The means we use to ensure that our *deliverables* are produced to the designed standards.

Quality control – The process of checking that *deliverables* meet the required standards before we release them to our client.

Quality design – The process of getting the right quality into the *specifications* and design of the *deliverables*.

RACI chart – A form of *responsibility chart*, where RACI stands for four common roles of: responsible, authority, consulted and informed.

RAG status – Status *report* that allocates red, amber or green status to *project* activities depending upon their performance – from good performance, according to *plan* (green), to poor performance that deviates substantially (red).

Report – The two types of report we produce in the Delivery stage are: *progress reports*, also known as highlight reports, summary reports or project updates, and *exception reports*.

Request for change – Formal proposal that change is made to the *scope* or *objectives* of the *project*, or to the *specification* of one or more of the *deliverables*.

Requirements – What customers, clients or users need from your *project*. These can be both quality- and functionally-driven. To help prioritise these, we use *MoSCoW* analysis.

Responsibility charts – Powerful tools for planning what people we need and how we will use them. The two common forms are the *RACI chart* and the *responsibility grid*, which is more formally known as the *linear responsibility chart (LRC)*.

Responsibility grid – More formally known as the *linear responsibility chart (LRC)*.

Risk – *Project* risk is uncertainty that can affect *outcomes*. Risk can introduce a positive (opportunity) or negative (*threat*) change. The level of uncertainty is measured by the *likelihood* or probability of the risk and the effect on outcomes is measured by its *impact* or sometimes severity. The latter term, however, only implies the scale of the impact, whilst the term 'impact' captures both the severity and nature of the effect. We tend to focus on threats – risks with a negative impact.

Risk appetite – The level of exposure to *risk* that you are prepared to tolerate.

Risk management – A vital aspect of *project management* that recognises the importance of anticipating and dealing proactively with the things that could go wrong.

Risk register – Formal document and management tool that records all *risks* identified by the project *team*, along with the team's assessment of the risks, plans to manage the risks, and progress against the plans.

Scope – How much work we need to do and how much our *project* will produce. Scope can be expressed in terms of activities, articulated by the *work breakdown structure,* or in terms of *deliverables*, articulated by the *product breakdown structure.* An inevitable pressure, which *project managers* work hard to counter, is for people to add work to our project; a process known as *scope creep*.

Scope creep – The tendency for people to sneak extra work and outputs into the *project*'s list of responsibilities. Can cause a project to fail under the burden of additional work, without the corresponding resources.

Slack – Informal word, used to mean *float*.

Specification – Specifications define *deliverables* as precisely as possible. These derive from a good understanding of the *requirements*; both quality- and functionally-driven.

SRO – Senior responsible owner – a *PRINCE2*™ term for the *project sponsor*.

Stage – *Projects* are divided into stages, or phases, to help us manage them. In *How to Manage a Great Project* we worked with four basic stages: Definition, Planning, Delivery and Closure.

Stage boundary – Stages are separated by stage boundarie**s**, also known as 'stage gates', 'gates' or 'gateways'. These are review points where we make go or no-go decisions based on how the *project* is performing and the value we will get from our further investment.

Stakeholder – Anyone with an interest in your *project* – whether affected by its *outcome* or process, or with an ability to affect its outcome or process.

Steering group – The term is sometimes used as an alternative to *project board*, but steering groups are sometimes a different body with an advisory role, feeding their comments into the board.

TCQ triangle – The time–cost–quality triangle, also known as the 'triangle of balance', 'triple constraint' or, in the USA, the 'iron triangle'.

Team – A small number of people who collaborate to achieve a shared *goal.*

Threat – A *risk* with an adverse *impact* upon the *outcome*.

Traffic light report – See *RAG status*.

Virtual team – A *team* that does not work together physically all of the time.

Work breakdown structure (WBS) – Formal tool that breaks the *project* (the work) down into a structure – allowing a firm inventory of tasks, in a logical hierarchy. From this, we can allocate people to tasks, to create an *organisational breakdown structure (OBS)* and we can put cost estimates against each activity to build up a project *budget* in the form of a *cost breakdown structure (CBS)*. The *deliverables* can be documented in hierarchical format in a similar way, to create a *product breakdown structure (PBS)*.

Work package – A defined chunk of work, usually contained within a single *work stream*. We can allocate specific chunks of work in a formal manner, using a document called a 'work package definition (WPD)'.

Work stream – A subset of the *work breakdown structure* (WBS) that is allocated to a single manager, the 'work stream leader'.

Who else needs to manage a great project?

How many of your friends and colleagues are struggling with a project and yet don't even think of it as 'a project'?

If you know someone who needs to feel more in control of what they are doing and you suspect that it is really a project – or a lot like one – why not give them the boost they need? Lend them your copy of *How to Manage a Great Project*. Or give it to them!

And if you cannot bear to be parted from it, recommend it to them. Or, best of all, be a really good friend to them, and buy them their own copy today.

Colleague				
Project				
Strategy	Lend ☐	Give ☐	Recommend ☐	Buy ☐

Colleague				
Project				
Strategy	Lend ☐	Give ☐	Recommend ☐	Buy ☐

Colleague				
Project				
Strategy	Lend ☐	Give ☐	Recommend ☐	Buy ☐

Mike can help your team to manage a great project

Mike is a conference speaker and business consultant. He speaks at conferences, team events, workshops and seminars for companies, associations, public authorities and not-for-profit organisations. Mike also offers one-to-one and small-group coaching for people who want to speak so people listen.

Mike's topics include project management and the management of change, management and leadership, wisdom and personal effectiveness. For many years, 'Practical Project Management' has been Mike's most popular seminar. You can book Mike to talk about project management or another topic at:

www.mikeclayton.co.uk
or
www.manageagreatproject.co.uk

Also by Mike Clayton

Mike Clayton is author of eleven other books to date:

→ *How to Speak so People Listen: Grab their attention and get your message heard*, Pearson, 2013.

→ *The Yes/No Book: How to do less ... and achieve more*, Pearson, 2012.

→ *Smart to Wise: The seven pillars for true success*, Marshall Cavendish, 2012.

→ *Brilliant Project Leader: What the best project leaders know, do and say to get results, every time,* Pearson, 2012.

→ *Brilliant Stress Management: How to manage stress in any situation*, Pearson, 2011.

→ *Risk Happens! Managing risk and avoiding failure in business projects*, Marshall Cavendish, 2011.

→ *Brilliant Time Management: What the most productive people know, do and say*, Pearson, 2011.

→ *Brilliant Influence: What the most influential people know, do and say*, Pearson, 2011.

→ *The Handling Resistance Pocketbook*, Management Pocketbooks, 2010.

→ *The Management Models Pocketbook*, Management Pocketbooks, 2009.

→ *The Influence Agenda: A systematic approach to aligning stakeholders in times of change*, Palgrave Macmillan, 2014.

Index

steering group 70, 202, 215
Step Zero 18–19
support
    planning your 122–8
        resourcing challenges 124–5
        resourcing tools 125–7
        skills requirements 123
    sourcing your 128–30
        contracting team members from
            outside your organisation
            129–30
        team members from inside your
            organisation 128–9
SWOT analysis 50–1, 123–4

TCQ (time–cost–quality) triangle 21–5,
    200, 211, 215
team celebrations 195
team exits 184
team meetings 163–4
team spirit, fostering of by leaders 137
team traditions 137
team/team members 215
    communicating with 158–9, 162–3
    communication amongst 137
    contracting of from outside your
        organisation 129–30
    at end of project 192
    first meeting with 139
    focus on individual 135–6
    from inside your organisation 128–9
    reasons for involving in planning
        137
temps 193
testing 12, 179

thank you, saying 195
time 21
time value-based assessment tools
    60–2
time–cost–quality see TCQ triangle
time-resource chart 128
timescale 94–8
timing of project 94–8
traffic light report see RAG status

uncertainties
    and project definition document 36
usability 32

version control 166

work breakdown structure (WBS) 35,
    98–102, 106, 143, 202, 210,
    215
    amount of detail 99–100
    bottom-up or top-down 100, 101
    detailed work items 99
    key jobs 99
    making it mutually exclusive and
        completely exhaustive 100–1
    and scope 101
    work streams 98
work package definition (WPD) 132–3,
    203
work package manager 102
work stream leaders 102, 103, 215
workloads, balancing 124–5

you-me communication 162–3
you-you communication 163